Material 1
Marion von Osten

# MoneyNations

| | |
|---|---|
| Correspondences | EUroland |
| Former West | Sampler |
| Shedhalle | Border Economies |
| Media Networks | Counterpublics |
| Transnationalism | Migration |
| Webzine | Cultural Producer |
| Sozialarchiv | InterNET |
| CPKC | TV |
| Publics | Project Exhibition |
| k3000 | B92 |
| FM | Former East |
| Congress | Video Exchange |

# Contents

**MoneyNations**

"Free circulation not for capital only" read the flyer for the
exhibition *MoneyNations II* (2000) at Kunsthalle Exnergasse in
Vienna. The exhibition, part of a long-term research project
co-initiated by Marion von Osten on the subject of "EUroland
and the Economy of the Border," reflected on the role and status
of the post-Soviet region after 1989 in the "Fortress Europe."
The eponymous connection between *Money* and *Nations*
referred to the central thesis of the project: that the European
Union was to be understood first and foremost as a project
linking national and capitalist approaches.

With the Maastricht Treaty of 1993, the European Union gave
the go-ahead for the internal market, i.e., the free movement
of persons, goods, services and capital within member states,
and, from 1999, the introduction of the Euro as a common
currency. This new economic area was accompanied by a shared
asylum policy and the reinforcement of European external
borders, excluding many of the post-Soviet states, none of
whom were a member of the European Union at the time of
the *MoneyNations II* project.

Both exhibition and research project, *MoneyNations* aimed
to "approach the complex and contradictory process of
forming collective and individual in (radically) shifting political
conditions."[1] On the one hand, it examined prevailing
political conditions: how does the culturally and economically
legitimated European border policy towards Central and
Southeast Europe operate? What are the consequences of this
for non-Europeans? On the other hand, narratives developed
within the project by cultural producers from Eastern and
Western European contexts were intended to counteract the
hegemonic narrative of that policy. This occurred through
a correspondence network of cultural producers from Poland,

the Czech Republic, Hungary, Romania, Russia, Serbia, Bosnia and Herzegovina, Slovenia, Croatia, Kosovo, the United States, the United Kingdom, Canada, Austria, Turkey, the Netherlands, Switzerland, Germany, Italy, France, Bulgaria and Slovakia, who conducted research on various thematic clusters. The correspondents captured the changes in the cities in which they were then living. In this way, documentation was created illustrating how the capitalist economy and border policy of the West was impacting everyday circumstances within different urban contexts. The polyvocal narratives of the correspondents served as situated counter-representations to depictions in the Western media that, almost without exception, stylized post-Soviet countries as "hinterland to be capitalized," using images of poverty, historical kitsch, and various forms of racism.[2]

*MoneyNations* took up four thematic clusters to examine the spatial, geographic and social effects of radical market-oriented (i.e., neoliberal) reform policies upon post-Soviet countries, Western Europe's new border policies, as well as forms of resistance to them. The first cluster focused on the consequences of economization in post-communist countries and changes to the cityscape arising due to new trade routes. The second one analyzed political actors who had come to wealth and power as a result of neoliberalism's new modes of business. The third one concentrated on issues of gender and sexuality in the post-Soviet context, and the fourth and final cluster was concerned with EU border policy and its architecture.[3]

Research within these four clusters was documented through texts, archived research materials, videos, photography and installations, resulting in publications, websites, conferences, and exhibitions staged in multiple locations. First made accessible in April 1998 via the Internet ("InterNET"), in October of the same year a three-day congress was then held at Shedhalle Zurich consisting of a workshop with media producers from the former Yugoslavia combined with an exhibition. An exhibition at Kunsthalle Exnergasse in Vienna followed in 2000.

As a Berlin-based member of KUNCI Study Forum & Collective in Yogyakarta, Indonesia, Ferdiansyah Thajib, describes in a conversation with the editors, *MoneyNations*' observations on the interweaving of political and economic aspects in the collective and individual formation of identity in Europe remain valid; further, "the logics described have even mutated in terms of context, scaling and complexity."[4] But it is not just the observations that resulted from the project that remain pertinent–the cultural production methods tested in *MoneyNations* also have continued to be of relevance. They not only articulated a social, institutional and self-reflexive critique, but, insofar as they connected these critiques, also had an instituting effect, making a claim to the redistribution of knowledge, money and attention, and investing in new structures of production.[5] Our present engagement with *MoneyNations* raises questions: What forms might a critique take that adequately responds to today's power dynamics while simultaneously pursuing a claim to enact alternatives? What would a circulation of capital and resources look like that is not directed towards exploitation, on the one hand, and accumulation, on the other? What role might the specific border politics of the EU play in this?

**Cultural Production as Transversal Practice**

Both the topic and the methodological approaches applied in *MoneyNations* are linked to past exhibitions at the Shedhalle where Marion von Osten was a curator from 1996 to 1998. In the 1990s, the Shedhalle stood for experimentation with the "exhibition" format. Exhibitions often arose out of long-standing project work and were not considered an endpoint but, rather, a staging post within an ongoing practice. In its projects the Shedhalle was committed to working with practitioners from journalism, activism, and education, consciously shifting the boundaries between art, design, and research, with a focus upon research-oriented practice that not only addressed urgent questions and social challenges but also worked actively to formulate counter-narratives and modes of intervention.

Concretely speaking, *MoneyNations* built on exhibitions such as *Schnittstelle Produktion* (1998), *There is no business like business* (1998) and *SUPERmarkt* (1998), which all made use of the art institution to engage with economic and political issues.[6] *SUPERmarkt* is foundational for *MoneyNations* insofar as it investigated intersections between money, market and gender politics.[7] Equally important is the project *Alt Media Use* (1997), which concerned counter-public media production, its conditions of production and forms of distribution.[8]

Marion von Osten was central to defining the methodologies and topics explored at the Shedhalle, regularly reflecting this in individual and collective texts. With the collective *kleines post-fordistisches Drama*, she theorized a transversal cultural production practice that sought to elude the "economization of life."[9]

In the epilogue to her dissertation, "In the Making" (2020), von Osten sketched out the potential of the concept of cultural production in its applied criticism to neoliberalism and the way it abstracts the worker from their means of production and creativity from the social, political, and economic context in which it takes place and claims knowledge as property. Against this backdrop, cultural production was seen as a rebellious act against established roles—such as those of contemporary artists, exhibition makers, researchers and creative workers—in that it refuses fixed social categories or professional self-understanding;[10] a critique that is exemplified by practices around the Shedhalle in the 1990s.

She positioned the concept in relation to Michel Foucault's reflections on the task and role of critique, which he considered as "not being governed like that and at that cost."[11] This approach has almost become a leitmotif for her generation in that it expresses a shared desire not to ignore the ways in which they had been governed by the politics of a rising neoliberalism, but, rather, to recognize its effects and attempt to redefine a space for agency.[12]

A second theoretical reference point is Pierre Bourdieu's sociological definition of cultural production from the 1980s as a subsummation of the art field, the literary field, and the scientific field into the cultural field.[13] According to Bourdieu's view, work identities and school or university degrees don't adequately describe cultural production. For Bourdieu cultural producers do not necessarily require an education in the arts: culture can be produced by a great range of practitioners. By his definition, moreover, cultural production plays a central role in society, as it not only describes the world but also intervenes in it. Alongside Bourdieu, von Osten argued for a cultural production beyond concepts of inter- or transdisciplinarity, one that places the emphasis on creating a vision of what actors have in common when they produce culture in transversal modes together beyond given disciplines.[14]

A third point of connection is Gayatri Chakravorty Spivak's analysis of a Eurocentric understanding of culture. Spivak problematizes the way that, within an occidental perspective, the Western or urban cultural context is described as dynamic while in a non-Western or rural context it is regarded as static.[15] With Spivak, von Osten argued for a form of cultural production that takes its own assumptions about itself and others as an opportunity to "fight these habits and be in relation and try to change culture with one another."[16] For von Osten, this means self-understanding based on a notion of being a "citizen of the world," and where cultural production is focused on the need to enter into relationships with diverse protagonists rather than being regarded as limited to the Western context.[17]

With cultural production, Marion von Osten thus describes a method that traverses areas of responsibility, competencies and disciplines in order to make normative positions visible while at the same time building infrastructures that rattle the power dynamics between legitimate and illegitimate knowledge.

**The Publication**

The present volume is the first publication in the MMVO series. It has gathered material on the *MoneyNations* project in order to contextualize and build on it. The first part, *Reaching Out*, documents research trips to Bucharest, Istanbul, Sofia and Zurich and the conversations that ensued with cultural and media producers. This section consists of faxes and emails to correspondents or intermediaries where first contact was made, the project was introduced, and possible formats were considered. Exhibition views from the Shedhalle and Kunsthalle Exnergasse as well as images from print and digital publications show the research's materialization. For the second part, *MoneyNations Inventory*, the participants, events, publications and activities have been compiled in an overview.

The third part presents a discussion between Sezgin Boynik, publisher at Rab-Rab Press, Eleanor Ivory Weber and Camilla

Wills, publishers at Divided Publishing, and Ferdiansyah Thajib, who is active as a community educator at KUNCI Study Forum & Collective, under the title *Going Sideways*. This section examines and expands upon Von Osten's methods in *MoneyNations*, focusing on how the project arose as a reaction against the hegemonial gaze of the West onto the East and developed out of the imperative to work out societal contradictions after the Cold War's end. Central to this was the creation of a particular infrastructure as a material foundation for a self-organized discourse—a method that is also part of the invited interlocutors' respective practices. In various ways, they create discursive spaces to allow underrepresented knowledge to circulate. In conversation, the working methods of the 1990s are brought into relation to today's forms of cultural production. Not least, the conversation provides the opportunity to share things, to discuss and make connections; it's a form of practice-orientated knowledge production that's open and dynamic. It offers space for different, perhaps even divergent, interests and ultimately follows our desire to reach out.


**The MMVO Series**

Based on archival research, the series presents material on projects by cultural producer Marion von Osten who passed away in 2020, contextualizing them through new contributions.

A central partner of the series is the micro-organization Center for Post-Colonial Knowledge and Culture (CPKC) in Berlin, which Von Osten co-founded as part of the project *In the Desert of Modernity* (2008). Developed as part of a long-term collaboration between Labor k3000 in Zurich and the activist group Kanak Attak in Berlin, CPKC provides an infrastructure for "intersectional forms of production beyond the limitations of temporal project frames, institutional conditions, publication deadlines and formally organized events."[18] The organization is currently developing an online archive that serves as a resource on strategies and practices of counter-narration and makes projects by participating groups and related practitioners accessible. The series accompanies this process of creating an online resource.

Inspired by the uncategorizable nature of Von Osten's work, its resistance to disciplinary confinement and its ceaseless negotiation of borders and boundaries, the series aims to elaborate on Von Osten's methods and practices. In its historical examination, the series at the same time remains committed to this very uncategorizability. It traces the outlines of individual projects in various media and formats, even where these tend to appear blurred, defined by the interweaving of relationships through friendship, research and production. In this sense, the individual titles in the series, each dealing with one of Von Osten's projects, will always remain partial and incomplete. At the same time, this publication's serial form is intended to make interrelationships between her different projects more apparent. The MMVO series creates access to materials for them to be used and shared.

1 Marion von Osten, "MoneyNations. EUroland und die Ökonomie der Grenze," *transversal texts*, September, 2000, https://transversal.at/transversal/1100/von-osten/de (accessed January 16, 2024).

2 Cf. Marion von Osten to Annette Schindler, The Swiss Institute New York, Center for Post-colonial Knowledge and Culture (CPKC), Berlin.

3 Cf. ibid.

4 Sezgin Boynik (Rab-Rab Press), Eleanor Ivory Weber, Camilla Wills (Divided Publishing), Ferdiansyah Thajib (KUNCI Study Forum & Collective) and Lucie Kolb, Max Stocklosa, Jonas von Lenthe (MMVO), "Distribution First," in *MMVO1: MoneyNations (ca. 1998–2001)*, ed. Lucie Kolb, Max Stocklosa, and Jonas von Lenthe (Berlin: Wirklichkeit Books, 2024), 98.

5 Gerald Raunig, "Instituierende Praxen:Fliehen, Instituieren, Transformieren," *transversal texts*, January, 2006, https://transversal.at/transversal/0106/raunig/de (accessed January 16, 2024).

6 http://archiv2009.shedhalle.ch/dt/archiv/1998/ausstellung/produktion/produktiondt.shtml (accessed January 17, 2024). http://archiv2009.shedhalle.ch/dt/archiv/1998/ausstellung/business/businessdt.shtml (accessed January 17, 2024).

7 http://archiv2009.shedhalle.ch/dt/archiv/1998/ausstellung/supermarkt/supermarktdt.shtml (accessed January 17, 2024).

8 http://archiv2009.shedhalle.ch/dt/archiv/1997/ausstellung/alt/altdt.shtml (accessed: 17.1.2024).

9 kleines postfordistisches Drama (kpD), "The Precarization of Cultural Producers and the Missing 'Good Life,'" *transversal texts*, June, 2005, https://transversal.at/transversal/0406/kpd/de?hl=kleines%20postfordistisches (accessed February 7, 2024).

10 Marion von Osten, "In the Making: Traversing the project exhibition *In the Desert of Modernity: Colonial Planning and After*," PhD Diss. (Lund University, 2018), 197–98. https://lucris.lub.lu.se/ws/portalfiles/portal/42117484/In_the_Making_PhD_Marion_von_Osten.pdf (accessed January 17, 2024). 197.

11 Michel Foucault, "What is Critique?" in *The Politics of Truth*, ed. Sylvère Lotringer and Lysa Hochroth (New York: Semiotext(e), 1997 [1978]), 23–82, 29.

12 Von Osten, "In the Making …," 198.

13 Pierre Bourdieu, *Language and Symbolic Power* (Cambridge: Polity Press, 1991).

14 Von Osten, "In the Making …," 200.

15 Gayatri Chakravorty Spivak , "Culture Alive," *Theory, Culture and Society* 23 no. 2–3 (2006): 359.

16 Von Osten, "In the Making …," 201.

17 Ibid.

18 Ibid., 203.

## Material

*Reaching Out 1*
Video stills from Bucharest, Istanbul,
Sofia, Promachonas and Zurich

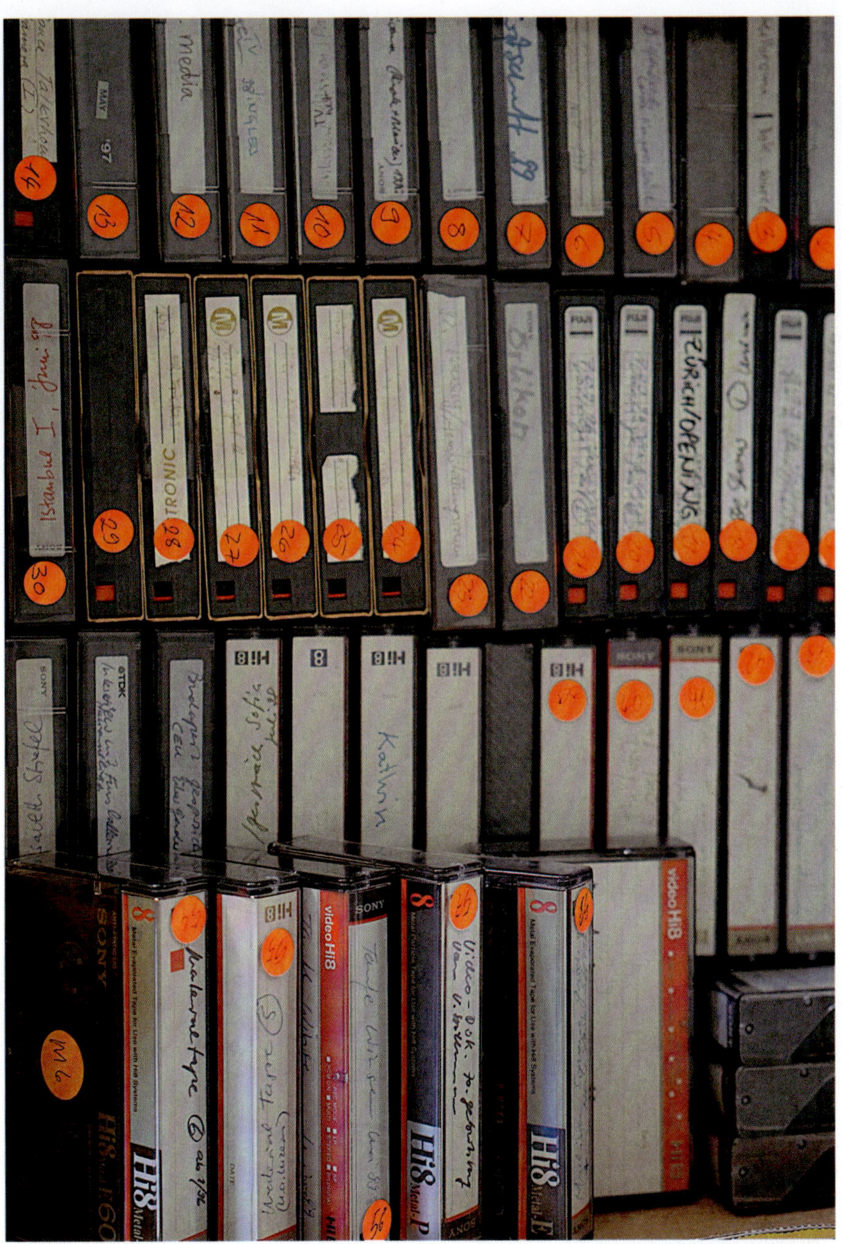

Hi8 videotapes at CPKC, Berlin

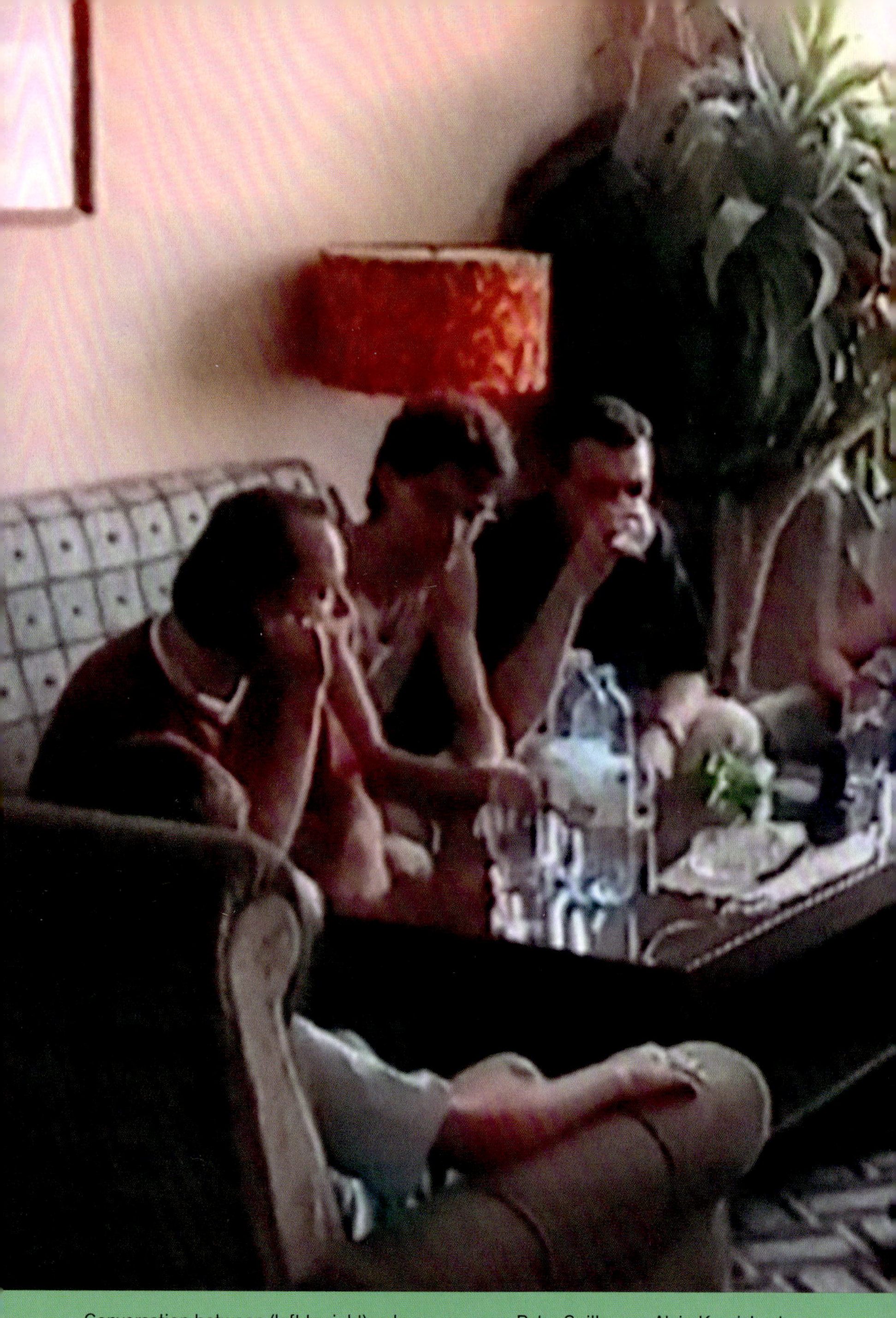



Conversation between (left to right) unknown person, Peter Spillmann, Alain Kessi, Luchezar Boyadjiev, Iara Boubnova, Marion von Osten and Nedko Solakov, Sofia, 1998

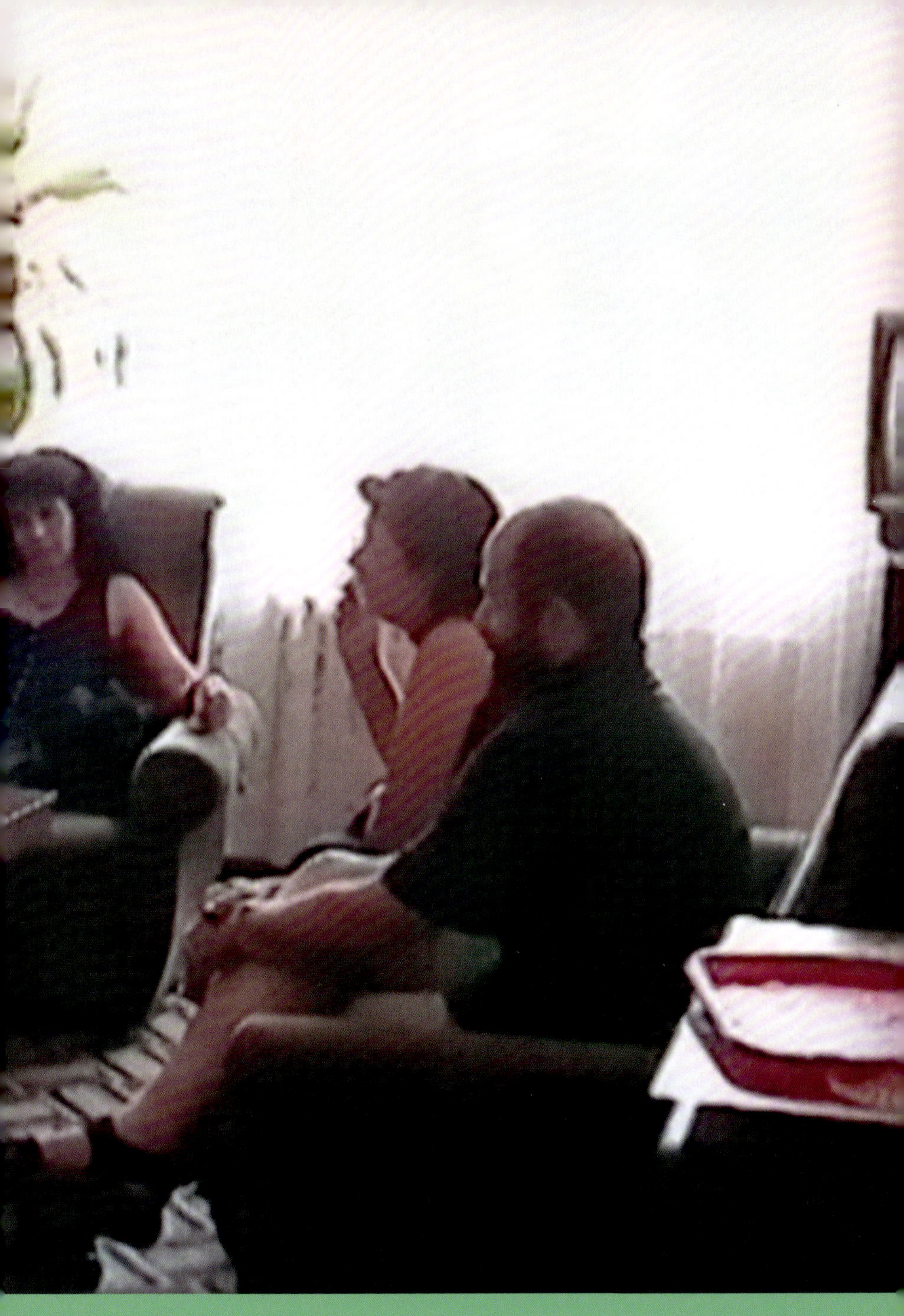

Video stills, Hi8 tape
Source: CPKC, Berlin (All images on page 20–35)

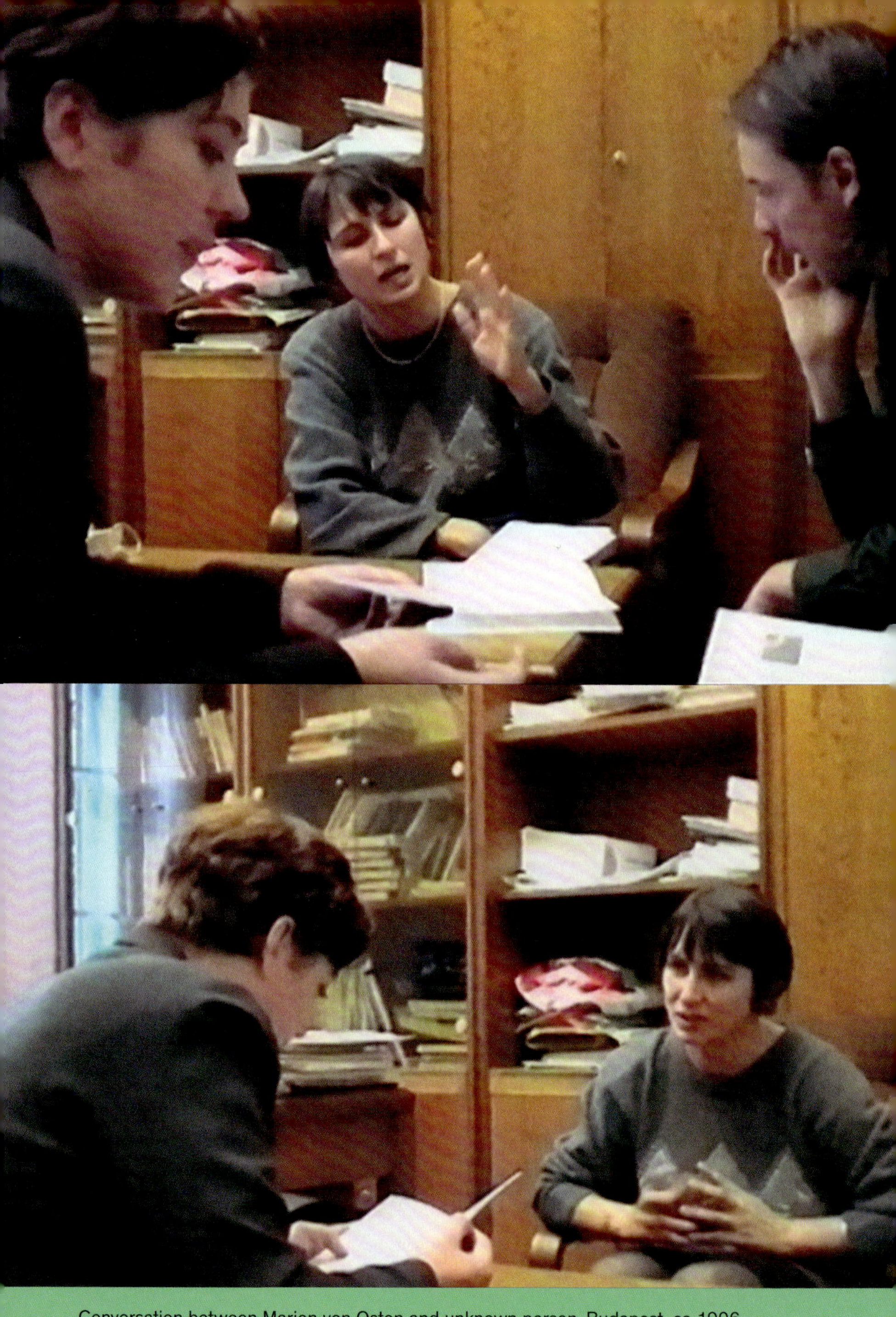



Conversation between Marion von Osten and unknown person, Budapest, ca.1996

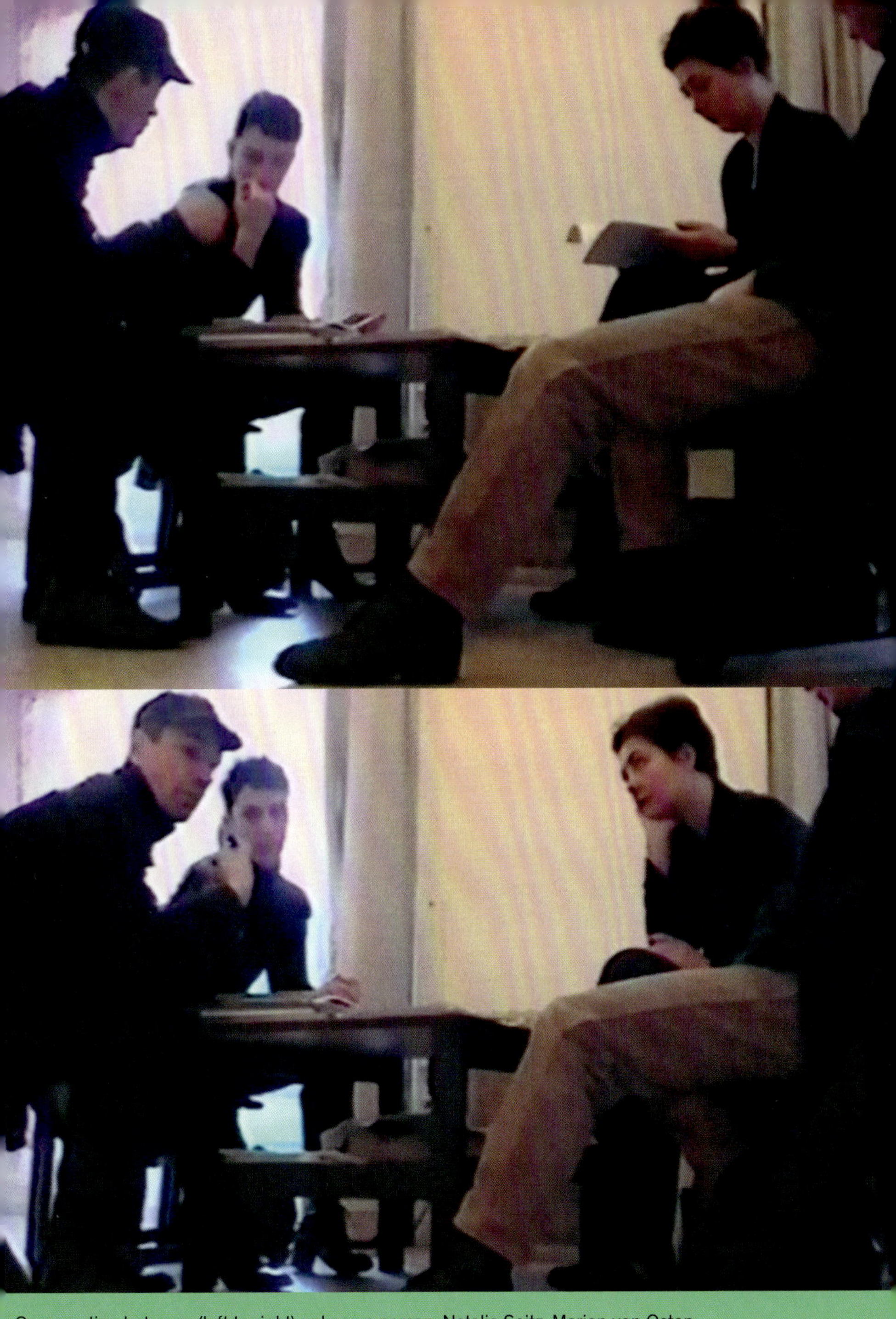

Conversation between (left to right) unknown person, Natalie Seitz, Marion von Osten, Peter Spillmann, Sofia, ca.1996

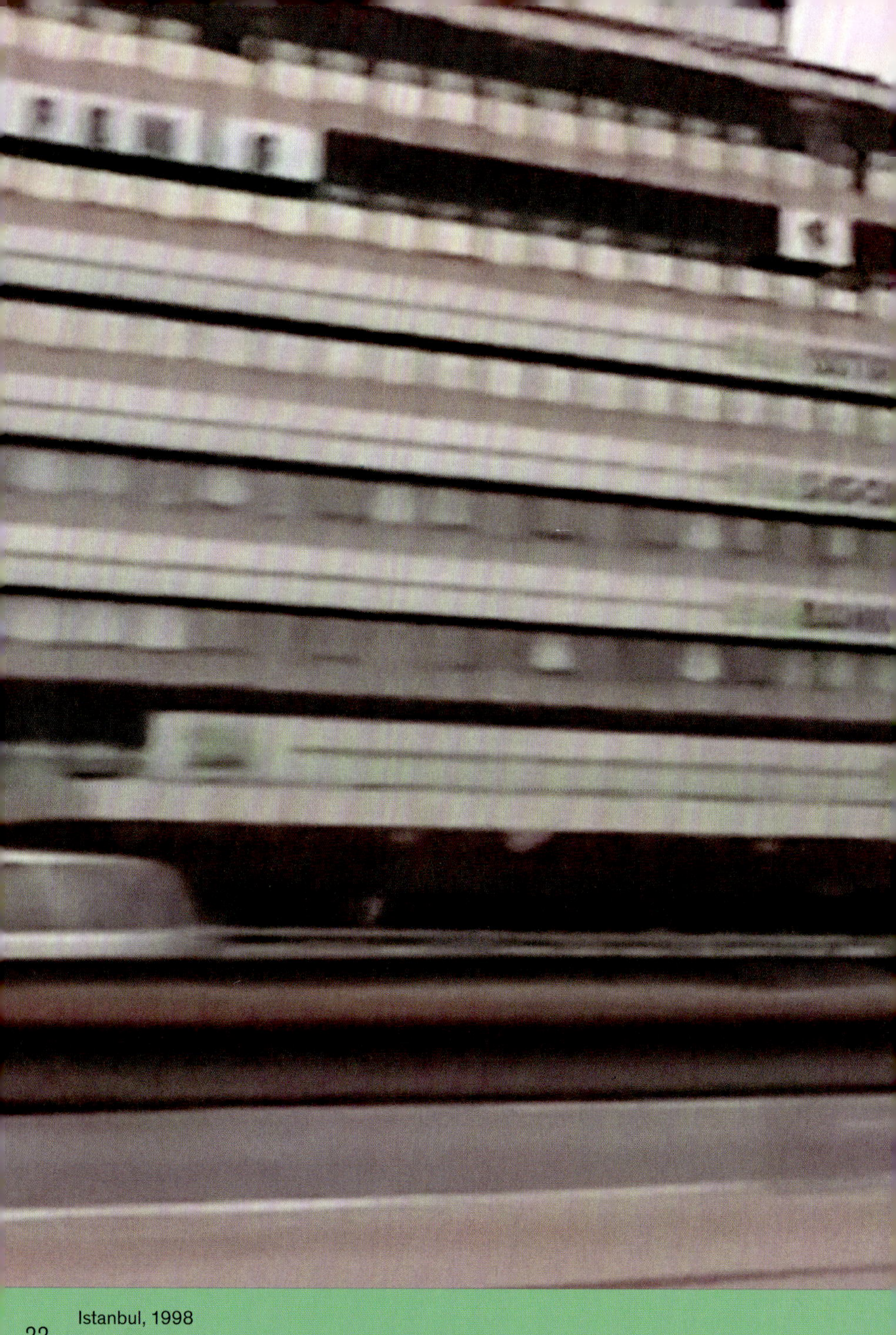

Istanbul, 1998

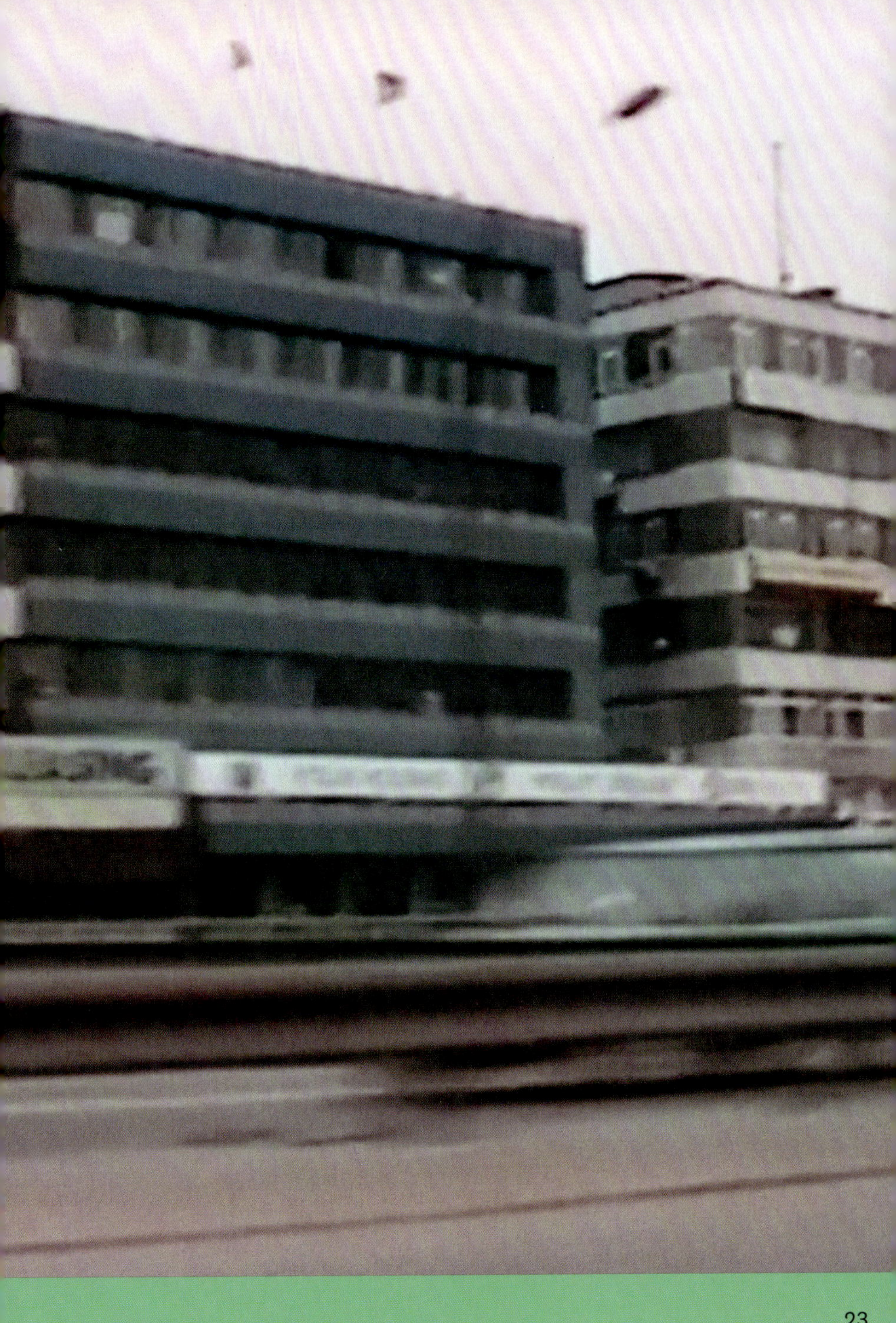

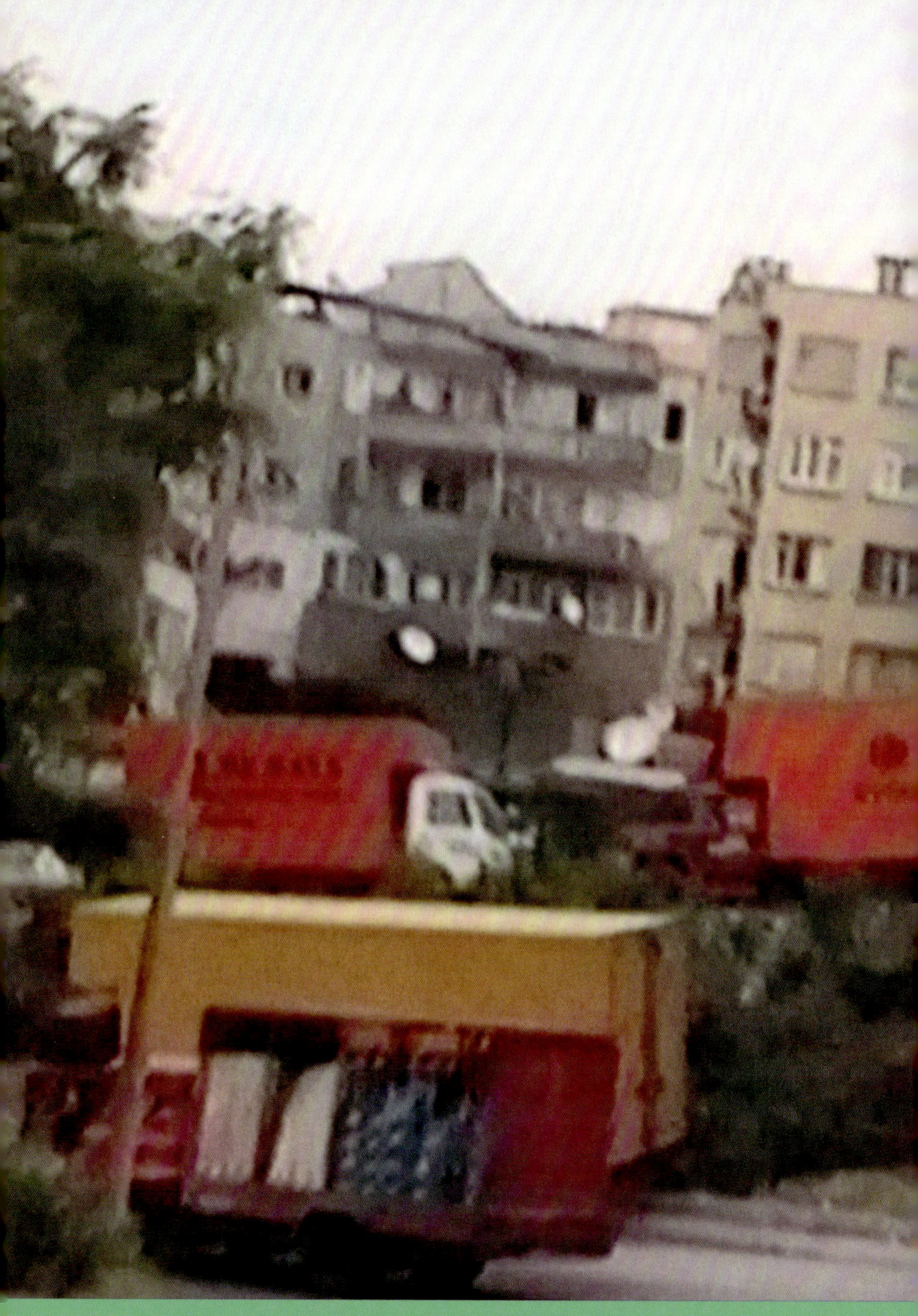

Istanbul, 1998

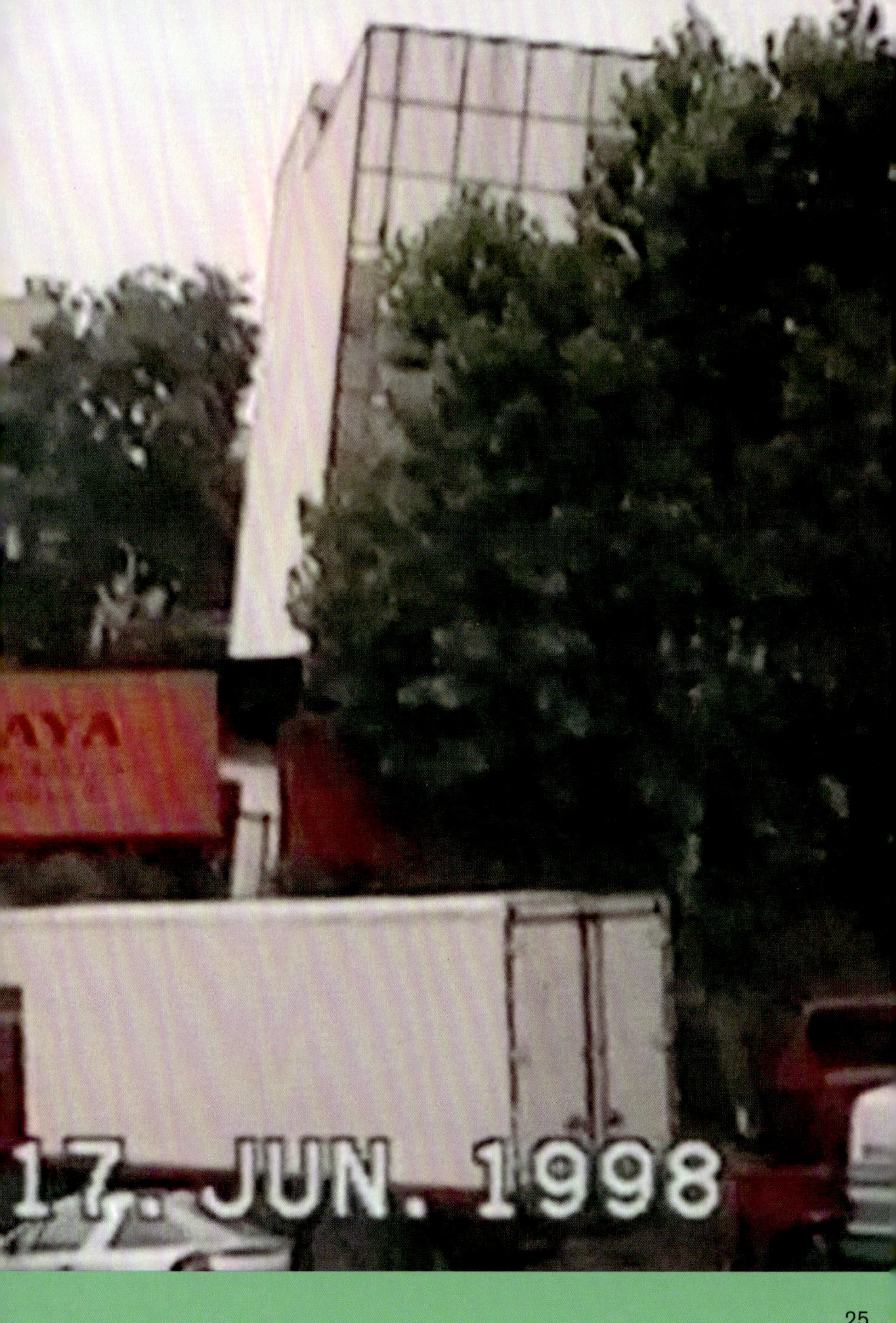
AYA
17. JUN. 1998

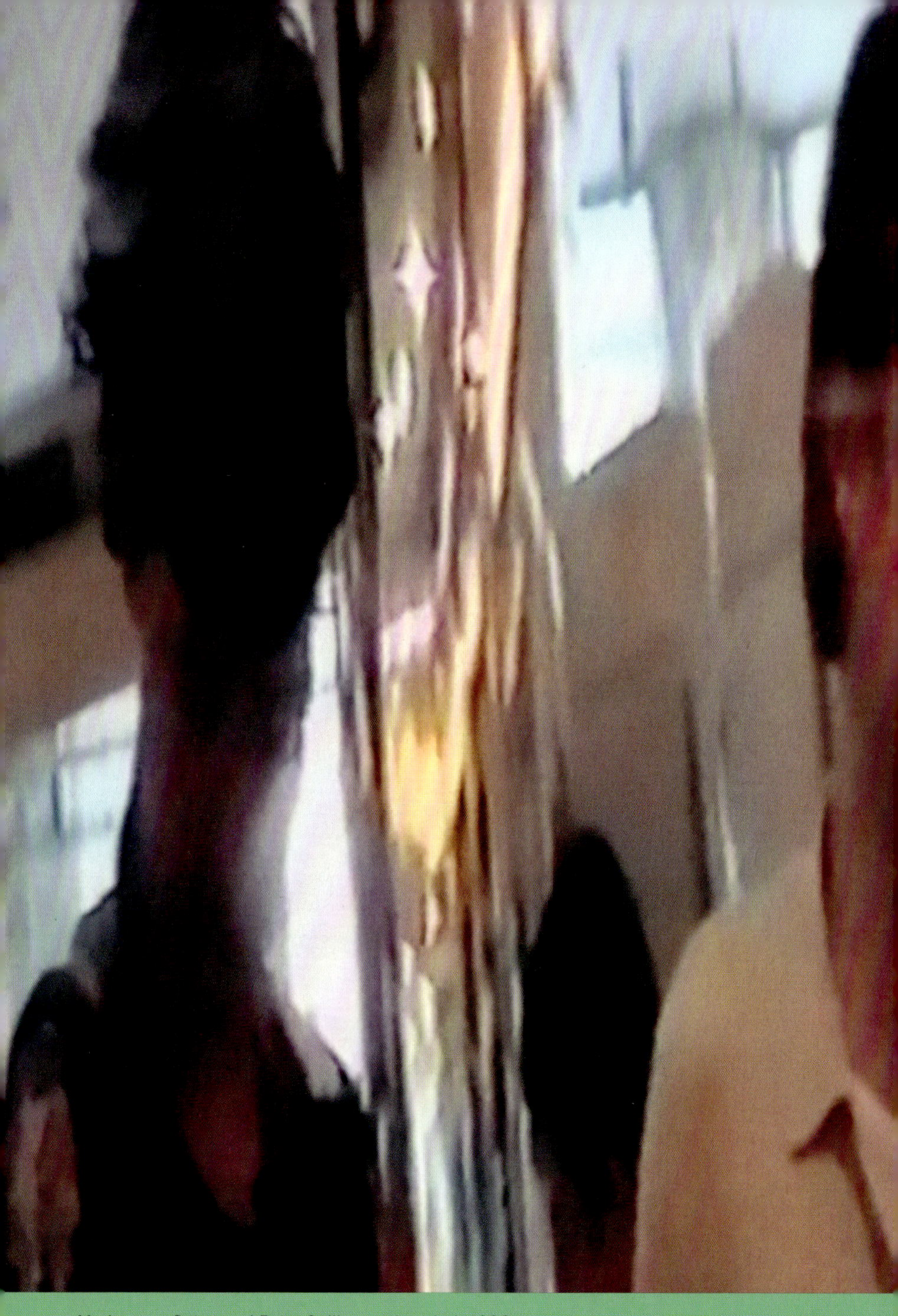

Marion von Osten and Peter Spillmann, Istanbul, 1998

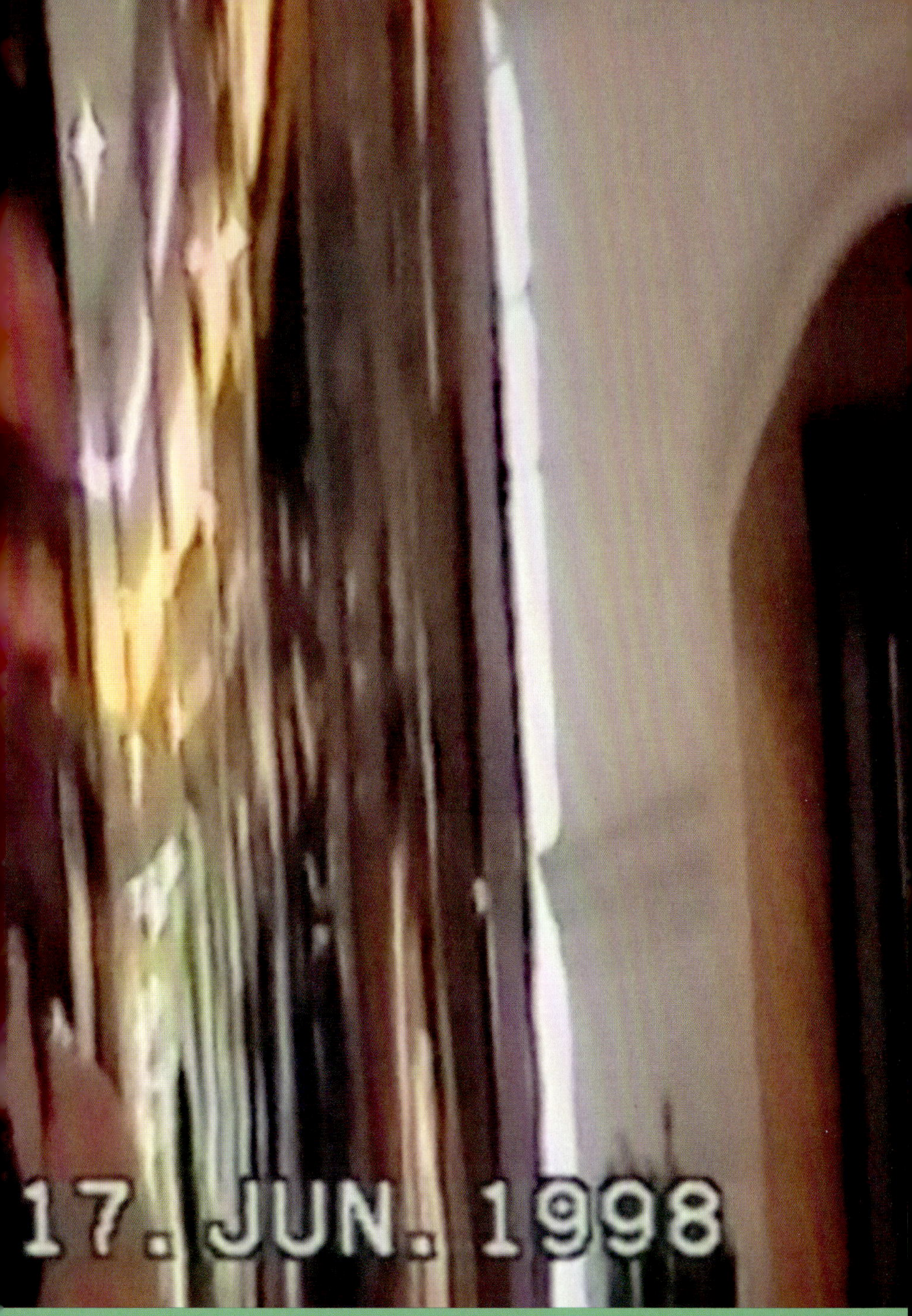

17. JUN. 1998

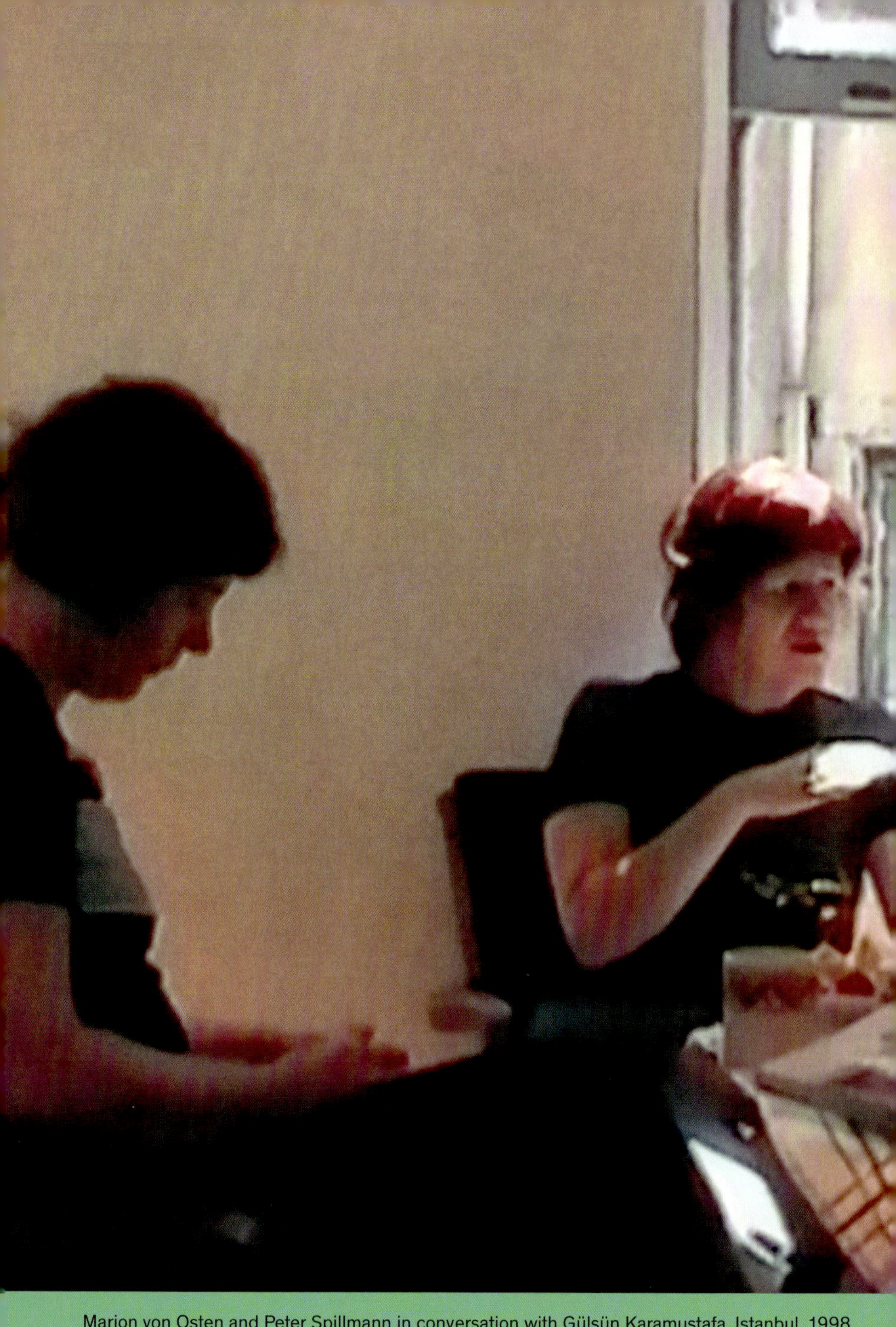

Marion von Osten and Peter Spillmann in conversation with Gülsün Karamustafa, Istanbul, 1998

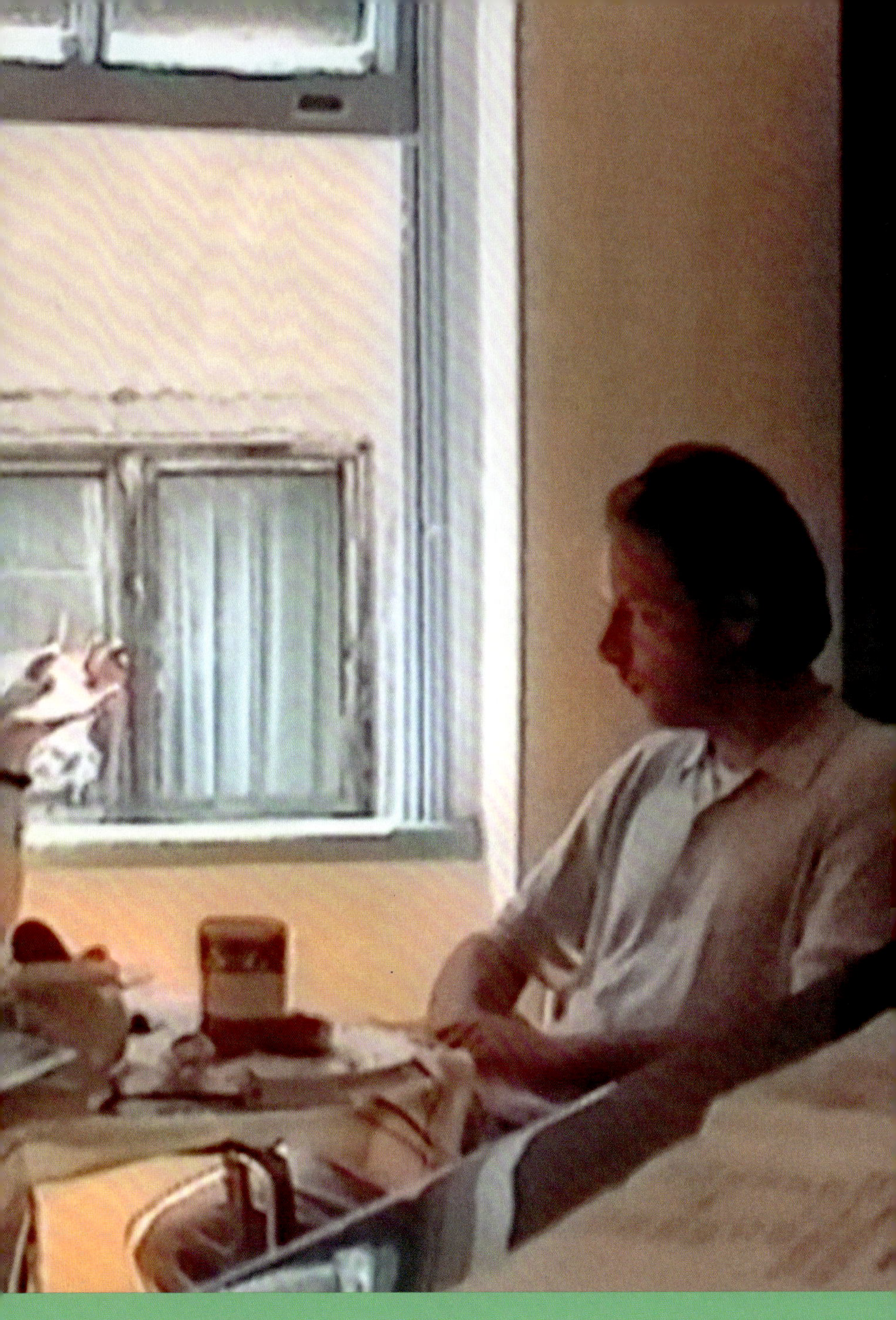

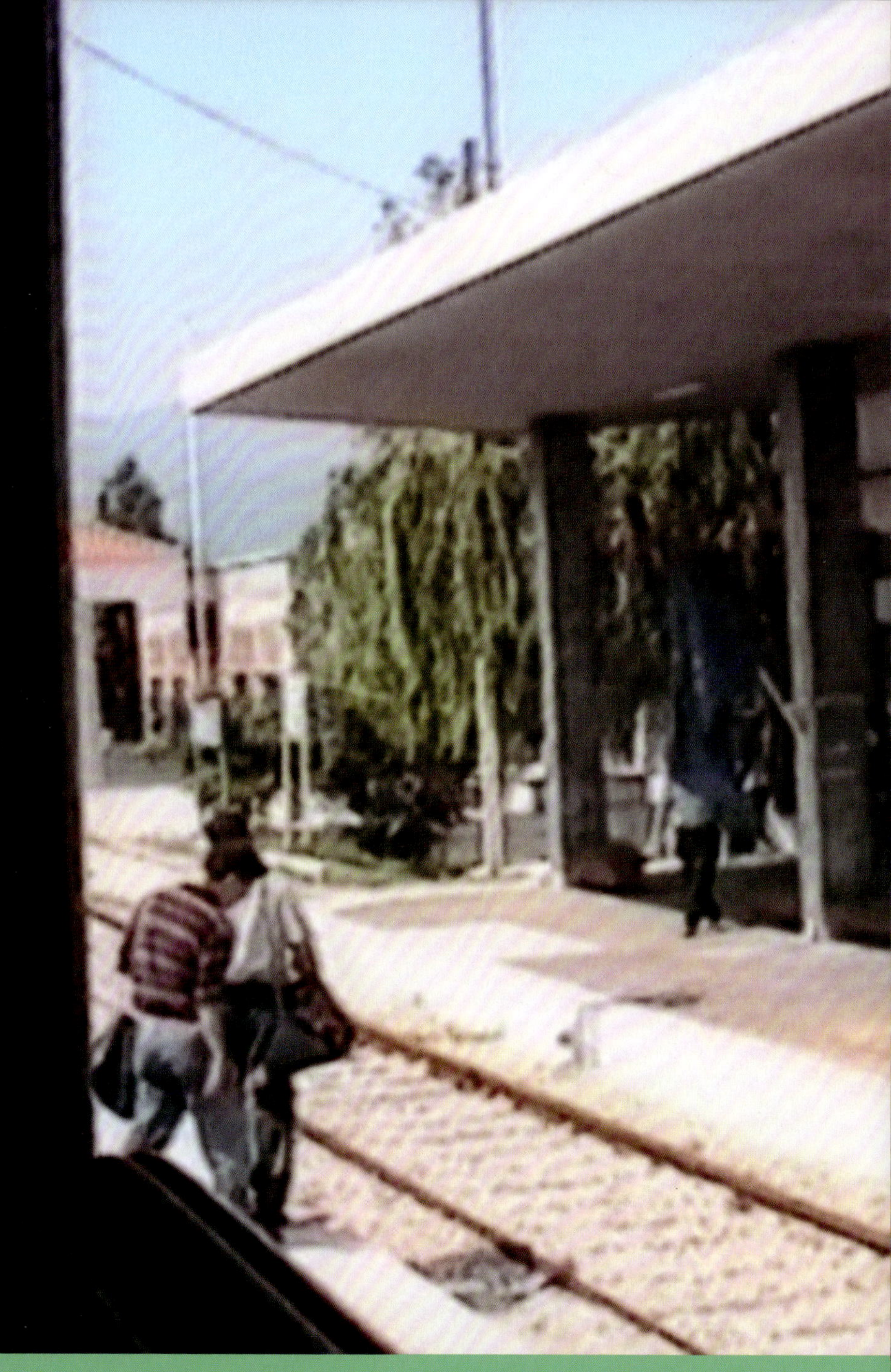

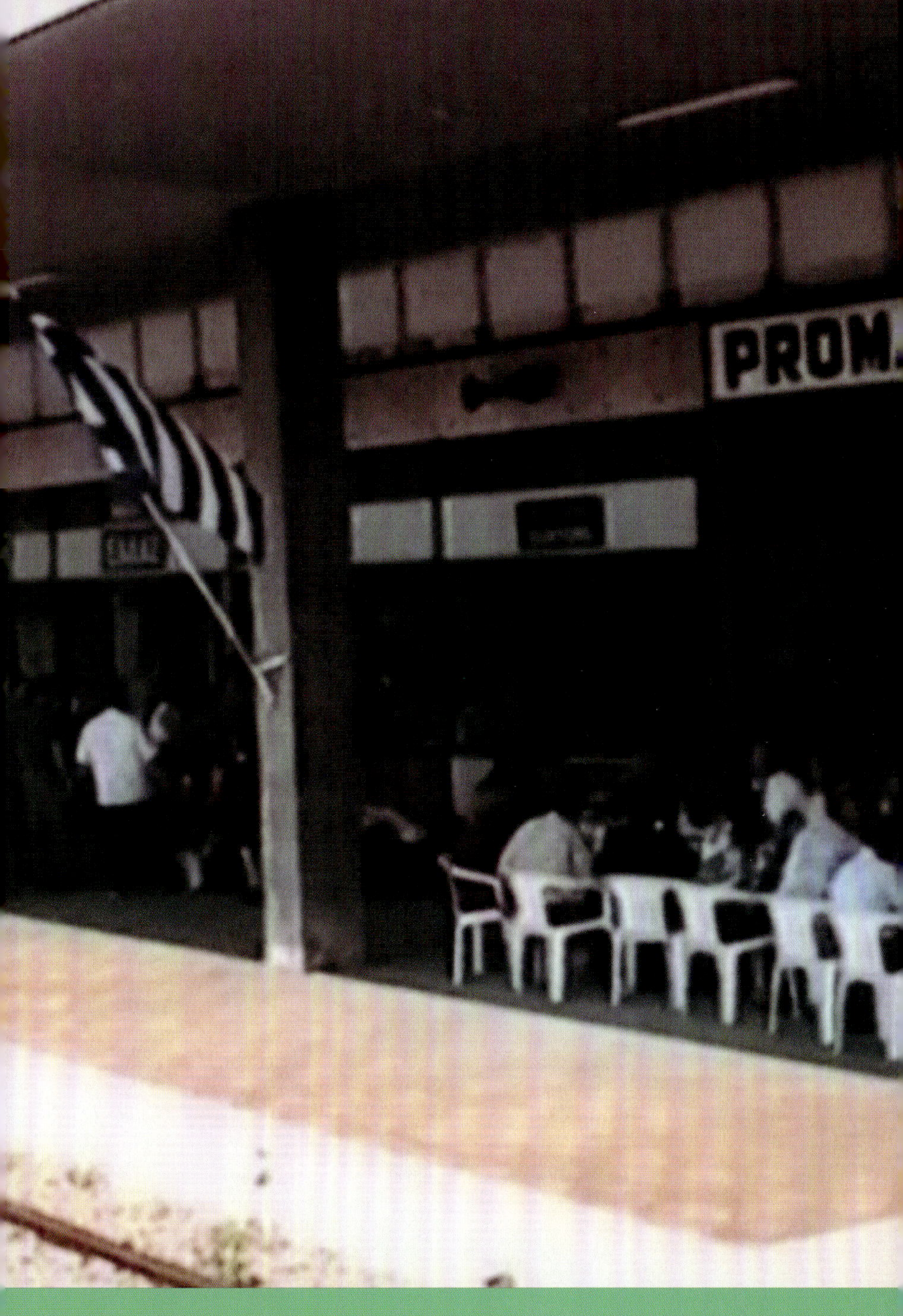

PROM

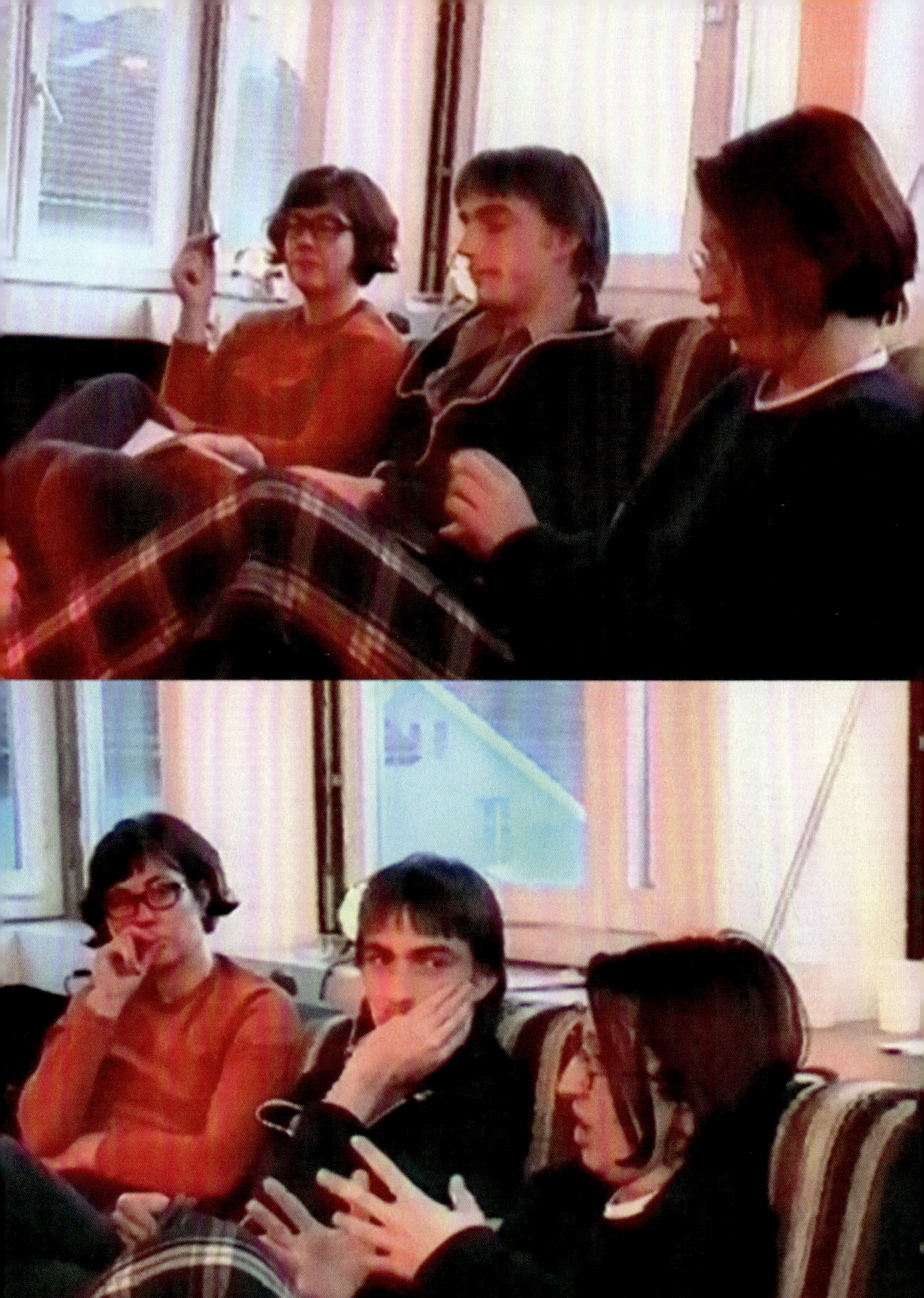



*Mediaworkshop* at k3000, (from left to right) Marion von Osten, unknown person and Jeta Xharra, Zurich, 1998

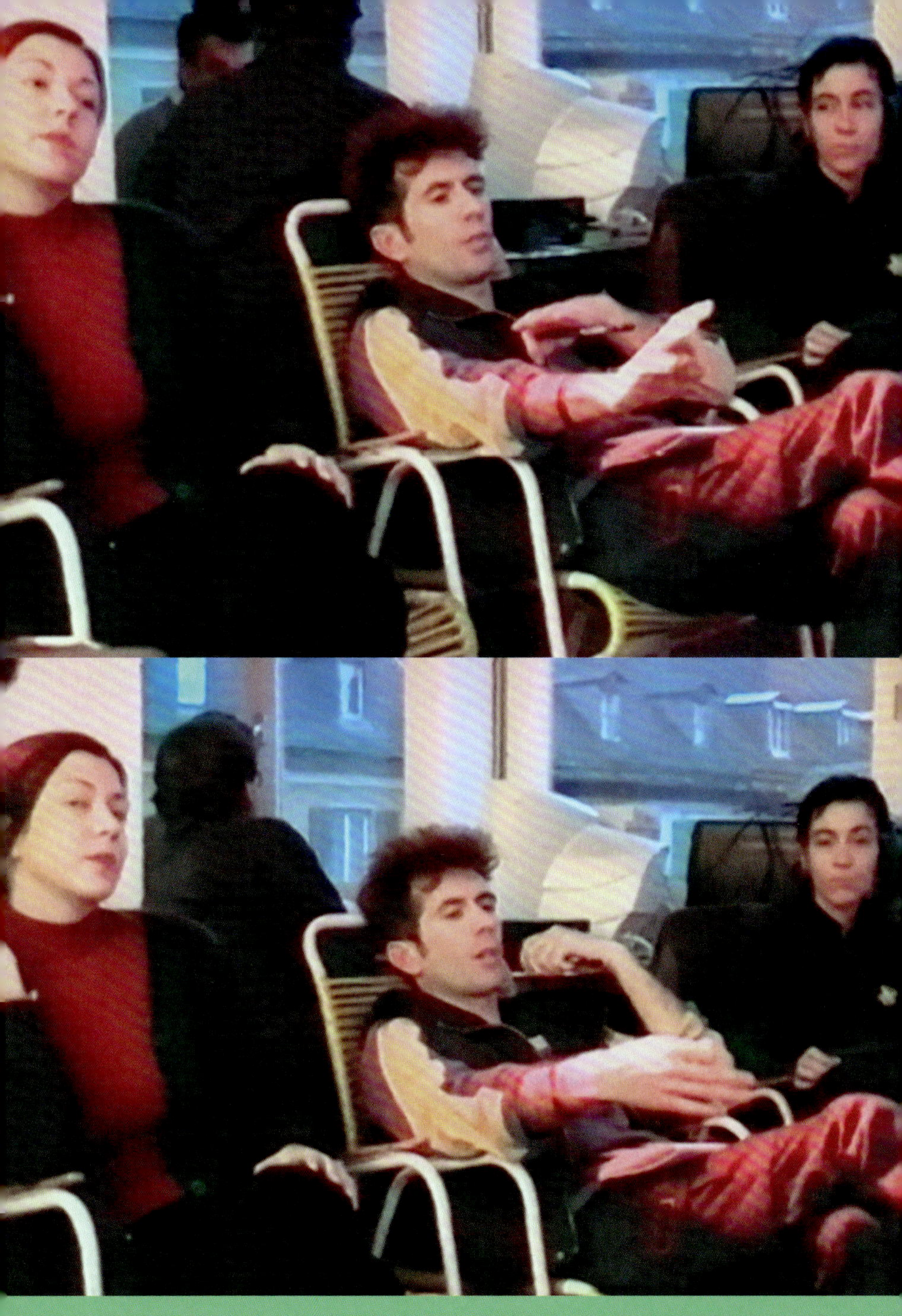

*Mediaworkshop* at k3000, (from right to left) Natalie Seitz and unknown persons, Zurich, 1998

# Material

*Reaching Out 2*
Faxes and emails

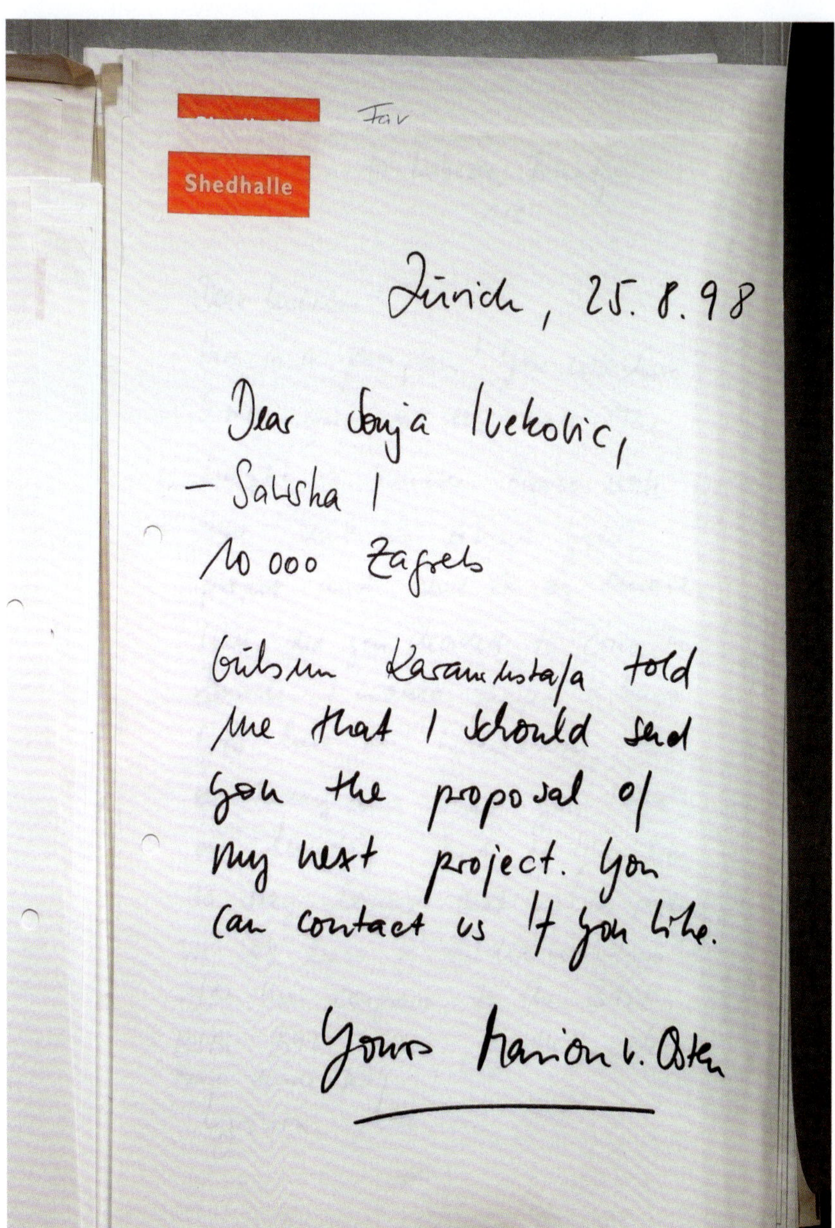



Fax from Marion von Osten to Sonja Ivekovic, Zurich, 1998
Source: Schweizerisches Sozialarchiv, Zurich

Dear Correspondents,

I think it would be good to give a short summary of content
of discussions that we are interested in for *moneynations* and
to explain how the Shedhalle is working and what it is. It still
seems to be a little abstract to most of the correspondents how
a project like this is organized, what its contents and aims are
and what the correspondents should do.

The Shedhalle
is a non-profit institution located in the area of the alternative
cultural center Rote Fabrik near the Zurich Lake. The Shedhalle
was founded by artists of the Rote Fabrik at the beginning of
the 1980s. The Rote Fabrik was first squatted as a result of
the youth movements and riots, but was eventually legalized.
Today, the Rote Fabrik is financed by the city's Cultural
Department and has several departments, including music,
theatre, studios, restaurant, and the Shedhalle, which today
is itself an independent art association. In the mid-80s Harm
Lux was the curator of the Shedhalle Zurich, serving until
1993. After that, the concept of the Shedhalle was revised by
the board. The idea was that the Shedhalle should become
a place for critical discourses in art and culture. In 1994
the curators Sylvia Kafhesy und Renate Lorenz were invited
to reshape the Shedhalle and they started a highly politically
and socially motivated program. In 1996, I was invited to join
the existing team. In 1997, the team changed again. I stayed
for two more years, together with Ursula Biemann and Justin
Hoffmann, who were chosen as the new curatorial team,
the position being limited to three years. The Shedhalle team
consists of two to three curators, a director, and an intern. Right
now, Agnes Bieber works in the Shedhalle as administrative
director, Nathalie Seitz is doing a curatorial internship, and
Justin Hoffmann and myself are the curators. This year, the art
historian Yvonne Volkart was invited to do a guest project.

Projects initiated by the Shedhalle since 1994 mostly deal with sociopolitical issues. The background to this discussion involves theoretical approaches referring mostly (just to name a few, even if it sounds a little bit strange) to cultural studies (authors like Stuart Hall, Andrew Ross, Frederic Jameson), gender studies (Judith Butler, Donna Haraway), postcolonialism (Gayatri Spivak, Homi K. Bhabha), urban studies (Saskia Sassen, Sharon Zukin, David Harvey), pop culture / music and post-structuralism.

In the Shedhalle, issues like genetic and reproductive technologies (Game Girl, Nature TM), censorship, revaluation of the PorNo discussion, or urban studies (Sex&Space, Kultur) were seen from a deconstructivist / feminist perspective: what it meant to use gender theory based on poststructuralist theory as an analytic category. All projects were unusual in method, because on another level they called the position of art or genius authorship into question. The projects were usually organized on a communicative basis, with artists, theoreticians and political and media activists. In this way, Shedhalle projects aimed at a new cultural practice, which could result in political intervention but also in new ways of theoretical and cultural reflection.

*moneynation*
The method:
a correspondent network:

The issues to be addressed:
What transnational accumulation means at the end of the '90s ...

Briefly, the theoretical background involves calling a materialist-based economic theory into question, because of the theoretical and social lacks it produced in the capitals and the socialist systems (paid / non-paid work, organization from above, gender segregation, westernization). In this sense, it is not so much the question of money itself that will stay in the foreground of *moneynation* part 1 in Zurich, but the political and social processes which are in a process of transformation because of the multinational flow of capital and the increasing power of stock exchange markets. These developments are discussed as the background of the new geopolitical situation in Europe and the new boundaries that have been produced socially, economically, and by migrations laws.

We don't just want to explain power structures more efficiently, but to discuss resistance and dissidence against dominant structures: with the issue of the "suitcase economy," how it puts the expansion of transnational accumulation into question, in terms of selforganization and as a subversive practice against "label" industries (for example in the textile industries). That will be surely one very important part of the project.

In this context, the "western notion of work" will be reflected as an exclusionary fact inside and outside the "West." To question it would also mean to question the ethics suggested by the distinction between paid work and non-paid work. Paid work belonged to the male white worker, the former cultural subject of socialism and the "hero" of the working class people of the West, too. This subject and its working conditions are very much in question in the post-Fordist society we are living in—and from a feminist and non-materialistic point of view it is nothing to feel sorry about. It is also of great interest who in our so-called globalized world is the cultural subject and what kind of a symbolic order does this cultural subject refer to (how is it gendered again, for example). This includes adopting a critical position towards the so-called "global artworld" and its meaning for the global economy, as it is part of the pastiche image of cultural hegemony that is always searching for new grounds—but to whom does it refer? (The nouveau riche? the service elite? the business man?) As you were talking about your TV interview in our last meeting,

Incomplete draft of a letter by Marion von Osten addressed to the correspondents, undated
Source: CPKC, Berlin

it came to my mind that the "new cultural subject" would be a very good point to start for you / us. The "crisis of the cultural subject" would also include a possibility not to talk about cultural differences (East / West)—as I always put the finger on, because I thought we have to get to know each other over differentiation. Now after the trip, I see it in a slightly different light and think talking about the "new cultural subject" would include differentiation, but not over a vulgar East / West opposition. What do you think about that perspective? Can you relate to it?

Dear Barnabás,

I think it is really no problem that I cannot have the full Budapest program. But there are a few people I really would like to meet: people interested in gender / feminist issues, because we should think about an art / gender panel in Budapest, for example.

I am very curious to get to know people from the Hungarian feminist movement.  I am planning a project in November 1997 which revolves around the question of the cultural representation of economy, money and the business world. Mascha Madörin, a feminist economist from Switzerland, the context artist Peter Spillmann from Zurich and myself started to work as a concept group together to find a different perspective on economic theories.

One idea within this concept is to contact corresponding people / artists in Eastern Europe who are doing research about the changes in the cities where they live, to get an everyday experience of how the western capitalistic economy changed the life sphere and lifestyle in this context. The other idea would be to find people / artists who are willing to work together with an economic theorist out of her / his country or city to find methods of visualizing the theories and critiques of these changes.

So, it would be good to find an economist who would be interested in this kind of exchange and to find two or three artists / filmmakers or also writers who are interested in doing research in that way.


I hope to hear from you soon.
Thanks a lot for your help!
Marion

P.S. Peter Spillmann and I will arrive on Monday, 28.10.96 at
21:12 in the evening, main station of Budapest. It would be
nice if somebody could pick us up, and it would also be much
better for us to stay together if that is possible. Otherwise
we think about booking a not-so-expensive hotel Monday to
Tuesday to Wednesday to Thursday night. Friday morning we
will leave for Vienna!

Dear Irina Cios!

I got your address from Peter Spillmann of the Viper Festival Lucerne. I would like to introduce you to a project which will start in different media (Internet, video, exhibition, conference) concerning exchange and communication between eastern and western cultural producers and political activists and theoreticians about the conflicts in the new neoliberal world order. Peter and I will be in Bucharest around the end of June and we would definitely like to meet you and hear what you are doing. Also, it would be interesting for us if you could introduce artists from Bucharest to the video magazine *INTERSHOP* which will be a counter-representational TV net and will be sent from city to city, of the participants involved.

I will let you know when exactly I will arrive in Bucharest. I will be in Istanbul from the 18th to the 23rd of June. Meanwhile, you can contact me through the Shedhalle email address: Shedhalle@access.ch


Yours,
Marion von Osten
Curator


Fax from Marion von Osten to Irina Cios
(International Center for Contemporary Arts, Bucharest), undated / Source: CPKC, Berlin

Dear Sirs,

I heard from Pro Helvetia about a symposium that will take place in Odessa in the next weeks. Would you please send me information concerning the symposium as soon as possible, because I would like to join you and go there. But I am leaving for Istanbul at the end of the week. Please send any information about Odessa that you have to the fax number 004114815951.

Also, I would like to send you the new project description of *MoneyNations*, about which my colleague Nathalie Seitz talked to you.


All the best,
Marion von Osten
Curator

Subject: invitation / B92

Dear Mina,

I am very sorry that you hear from me later than I expected, but I became ill and didn't go to work as I had to lay in bed. But now I like to give you some additional information about what we are planning in the Shedhalle Zurich. First of all, I think we already emailed you the concept texts about *MoneyNations*, but I am doing it again to be sure you have it in this second mail. What we would like to do, or what we aim to do with the project, is to establish a communication network, not only as a network itself, but as an issue-oriented information pool between Middle-Central and East European cultural producers and activists. The project includes several possibilities to participate on a textual level, with visual productions (both in the newspaper and the webzine) and videos for a special screening and distribution program. Also, real audio on the web is planned. The idea of the video network, to which I would like to invite you first of all, will connect critically working individuals and groups from the East and West, bringing together information about the social transformations and forms of exploitation occurring due to the massive expansion of international accumulation processes, along with their meaning for the political situations in these countries (and also for a politics of resistance).

I saw a list of your productions on the Net and I would like to ask if it is possible for you to send us samples of your productions. But also, I am thinking about inviting two people from your group to talk about your practice here, and your work in the media-activist field. But let us confirm that later, once you thought about the whole project ... It would be good to hear from you who we should put on the mailing list to inform other (media) activists, artists and theoreticians from the Balkans. As Geert Lovink told me, Lazlar produced a video about media

Email from Marion von Osten to Mina Vuletic (B92), undated
Source: CPKC, Berlin

and propaganda concerning ex-Yugoslavia. It would be of great
help if it were possible to send a sample of these as well,
because I think the issue of the video definitely fits very well
in the project frame. We will pay for all your mailing costs!

All the best for your work and I am looking forward to hearing
from you.


Yours,
Marion von Osten
Curator

Subject: Eastmediaworkshop

Lieber Reto,

wie ich mir denke, seid ihr gut auf Fahrt und ich kann Dich
wahrscheinlich nicht erreichen. Kurz nur zum Stand des
geplanten Medienworkshops mit Radio und MedienaktivistInnen
aus dem Osten (vor allem Ex-Jugoslawien). Eigentlich hatte
ich nach Deinem regen Interesse gedacht, wir könnten wieder
etwas mit LoRa / Klipp und Klang gemeinsam machen,
Radiosendungen mit B92, Videos mit terra aus Novi Sad etc.
Schon rumspinnend und freudig über eine Woche Austausch
und Produktion nachdenkend haben wir unsere Fühler schon
ganz in diese Richtung ausgestreckt. So fährt gerade Natalie
nach Ljubliana, und Sascha nach Sarajevo. Leider habe ich jetzt
allerdings eine Absage vom BAKOM von Herrn Rudin bekommen
und weiß nun nicht, wie wir es finanzieren sollen. So eine Scheiße
kann ich da nur sagen.

Ich versuch noch mal noch andere Kanäle anzuzapfen, vielleicht
hast Du auch noch ne Idee an wen ich mich wenden kann.
Anbei schicke ich Dir das englische Konzept. Das Internetprojekt,
das VideoZine und die Zeitung bleiben ja bestehen. Wie auch
der Kongress. Workshop ein anderes mal? Schade drum.


Gruß und keep on truckin'
Marion

Liebe Pauline,

falls Dich dieses Fax noch erreicht, so habe ich eine große Bitte.
Bei mir türmt es sich hier vor Schreibarbeit, deswegen wäre
ich Dir dankbar, wenn Du den Text von Correspondents schon
mal beginnst ins Englische zu übersetzen. Vielleicht machst
Du es gerade im Zug. Nimmst einen Ponds Dictonary mit
und dann können wir es hier vervollständigen und in meinen
Labtop eingeben. .... Ist das o.k. oder ist das die totale Hölle für
Dich? Bitte lege doch eine Kopie des Correspondent Briefes
auf Ursulas Schreibtisch und gebe auch Agnes eine zum
Lesen. Marion Baruch schicke ich von hier aus eine deutsche
Version. Dennoch allein schon für Gülsün ist es wichtig, einen
englischen Text zu haben.

Ich bin morgen von 11 bis 15 Uhr hier zu erreichen.


Ich freue mich auf Dich
Berlin ist klasse!
Marion

*Reaching Out 3*
Installation views from Shedhalle, Zurich, 1998
and Kunsthalle Exnergasse, Vienna, 2001

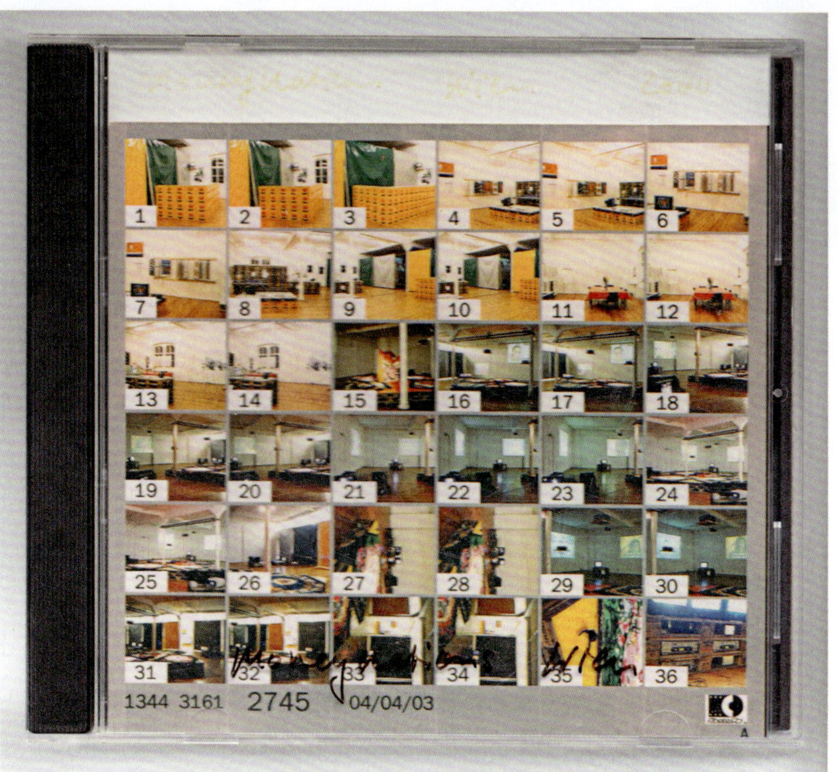

CD-R with digital reproduction of *MoneyNations2* exhibition documentation
Source: CPKC, Berlin

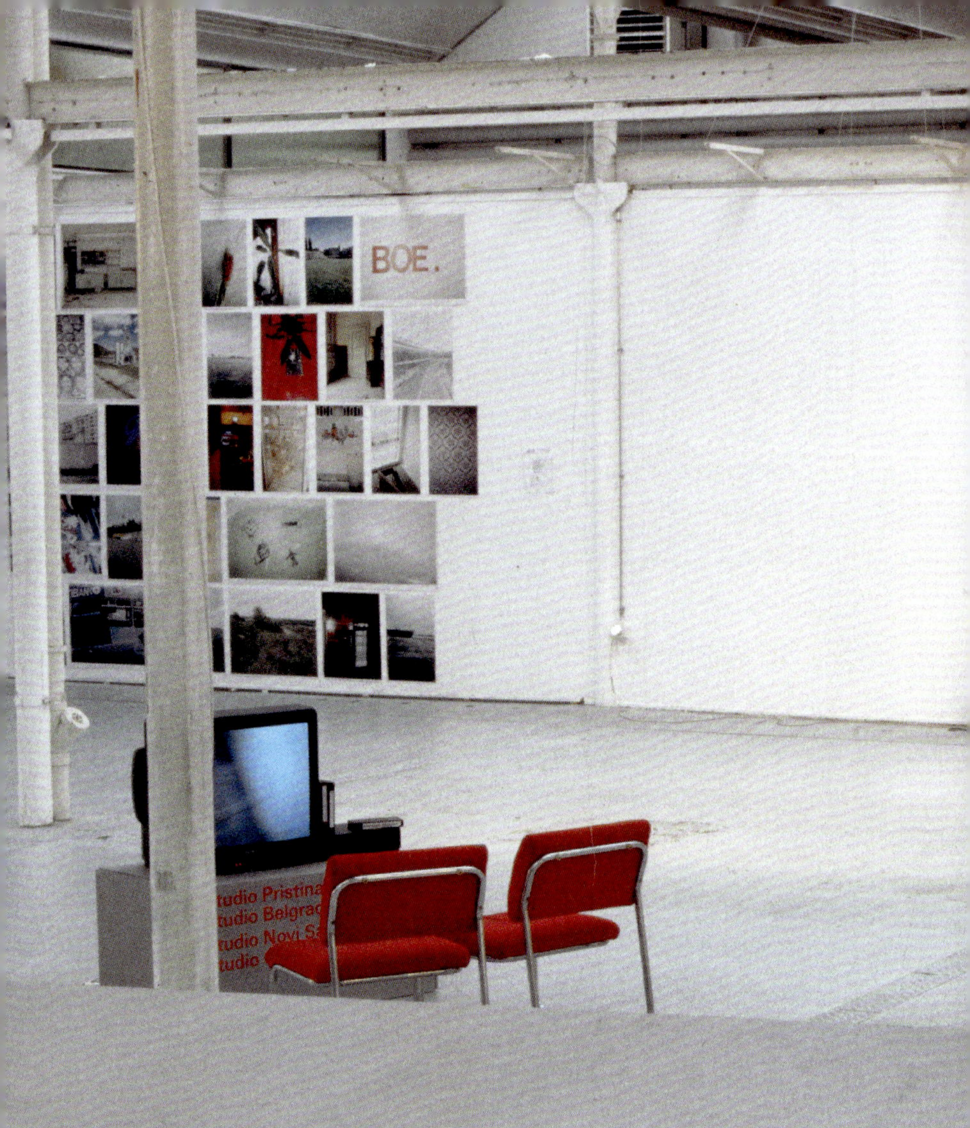


*MoneyNations@access,* installation view, Shedhalle, Zurich, 1998

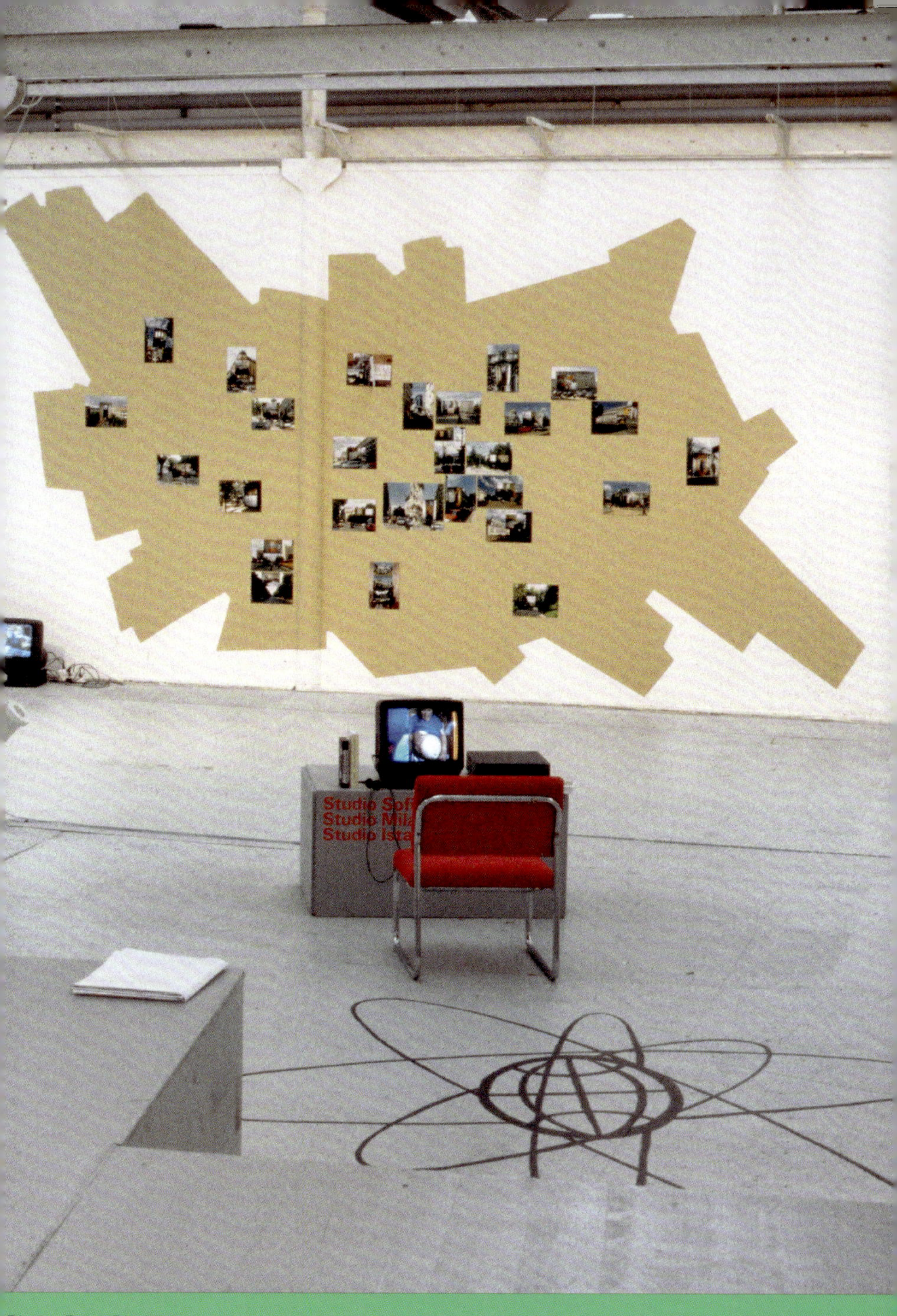


Photo: Peter Riedlinger
Source: CPKC, Berlin

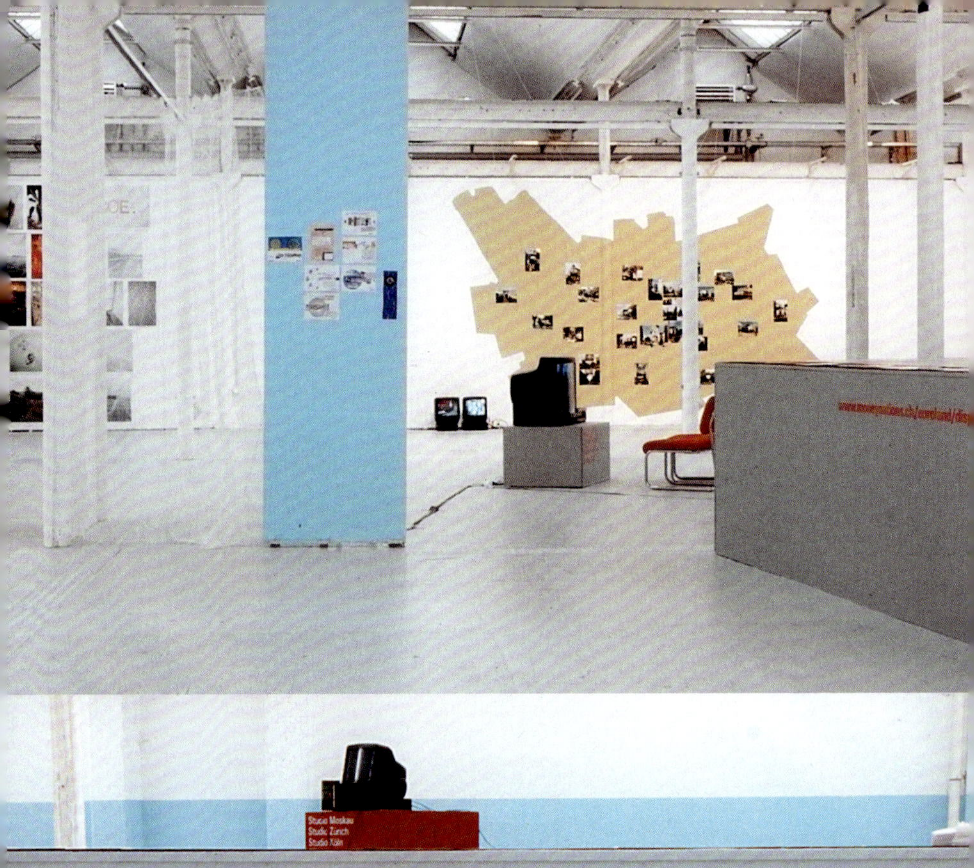


*MoneyNations@access,* installation views, Shedhalle, Zurich, 1998

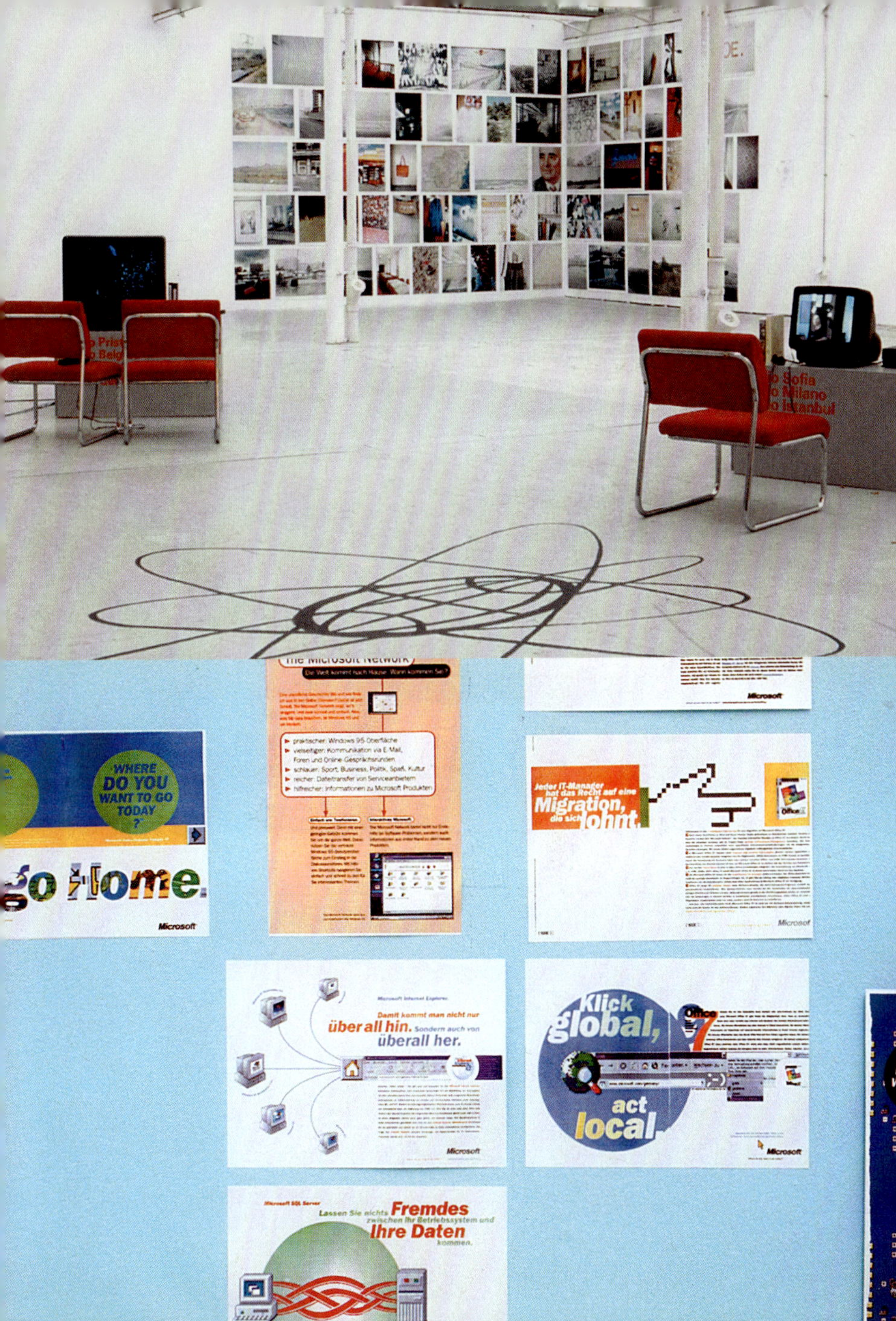

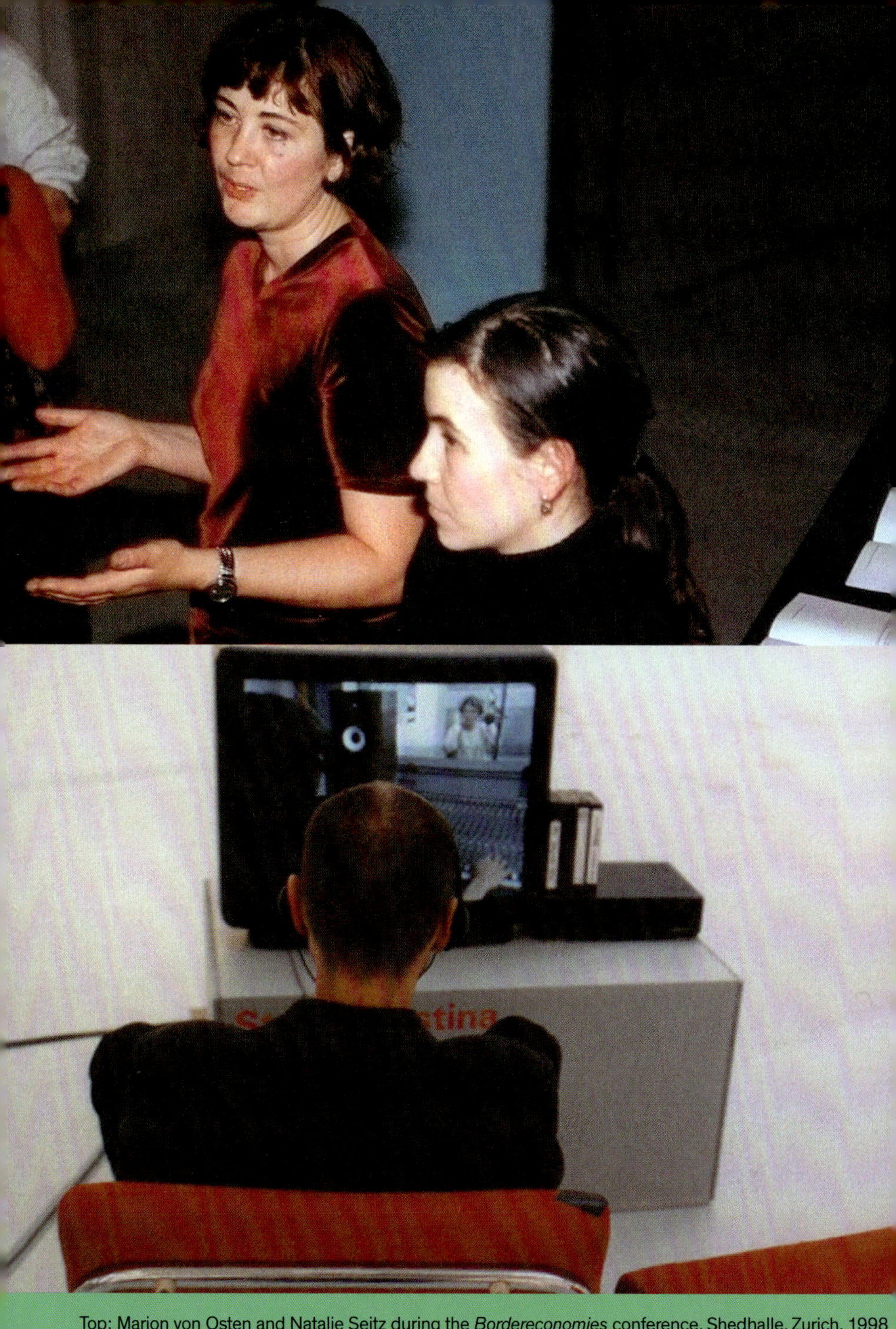


Top: Marion von Osten and Natalie Seitz during the *Bordereconomies* conference, Shedhalle, Zurich, 1998
Bottom: *MoneyNations@access*, installation view, Shedhalle, Zurich, 1998

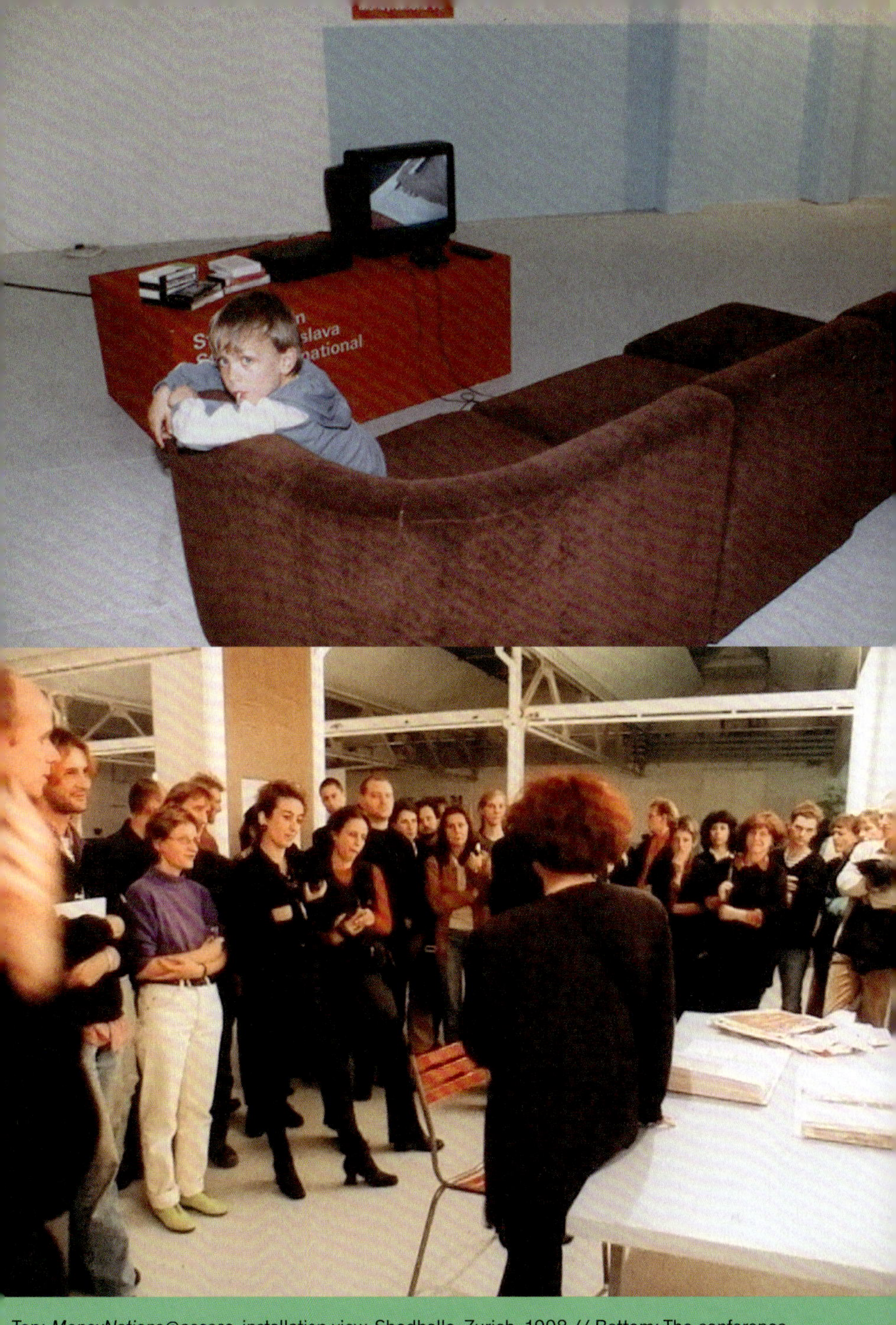

Top: *MoneyNations@access*, installation view, Shedhalle, Zurich, 1998 // Bottom: The conference *Bordereconomies*, Shedhalle, Zurich, 1998 / Photos: Nadine Podwika / <u>Source: CPKC, Berlin</u>

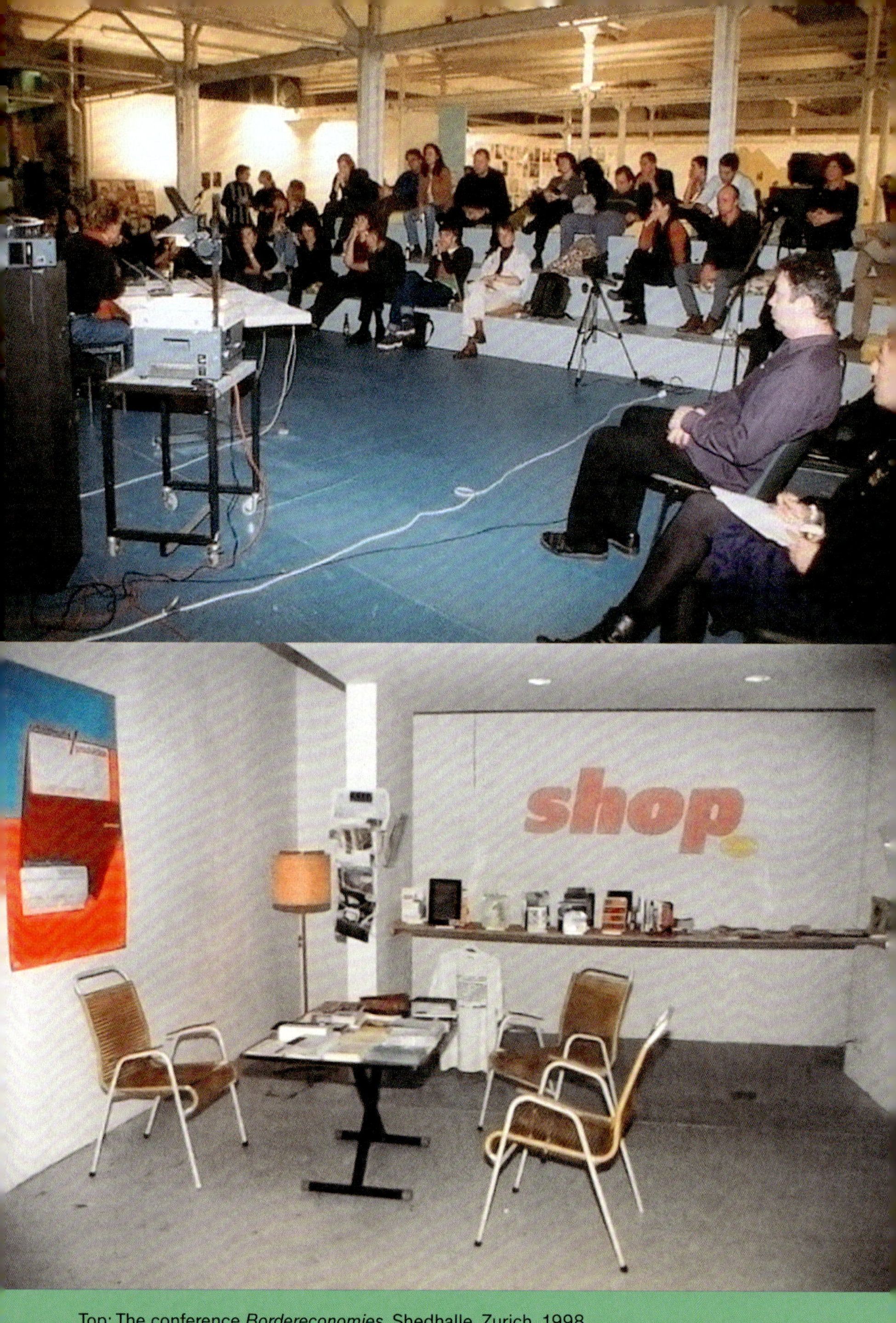



Top: The conference *Bordereconomies*, Shedhalle, Zurich, 1998
Bottom: *MoneyNations@access*, installation view, Shedhalle, Zurich, 1998

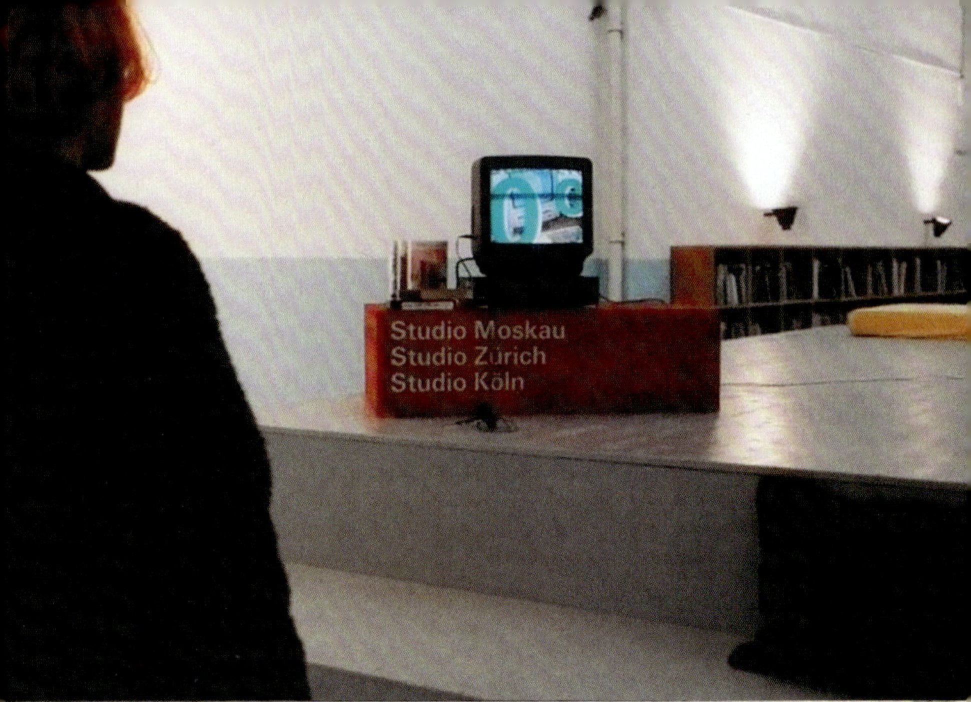

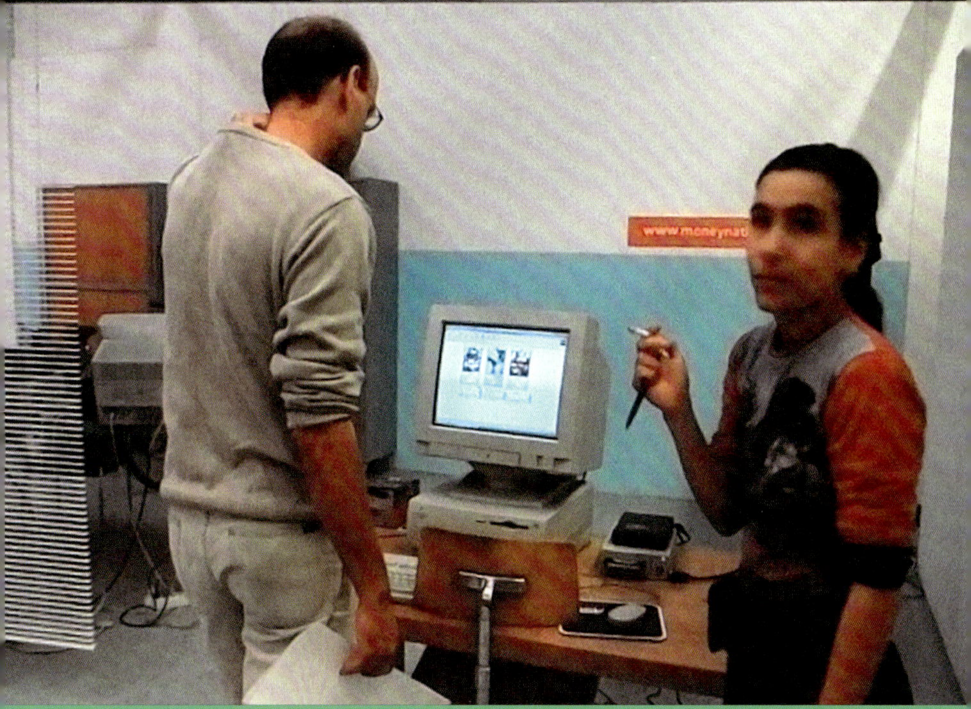

Top: *MoneyNations@access*, installation view, Shedhalle, Zurich, 1998
Bottom: Unknown person and Natalie Seitz / Photos: Nadine Podwika / Source: CPKC, Berlin

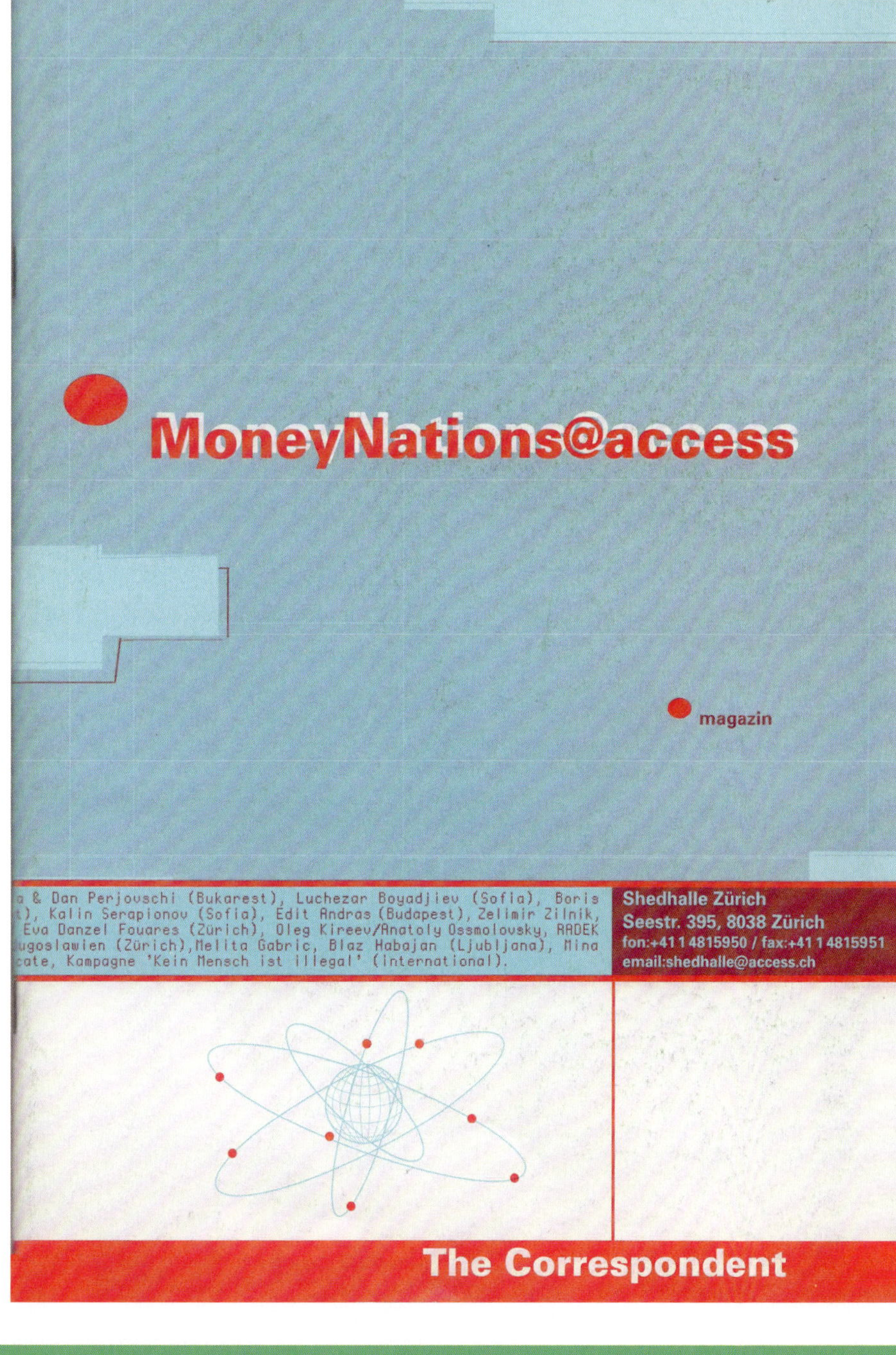




Cover and content page of the publication *MoneyNations@access: The Correspondent*, self-published in conjunction with the exhibition, Zurich, 1998

# The Correspondent

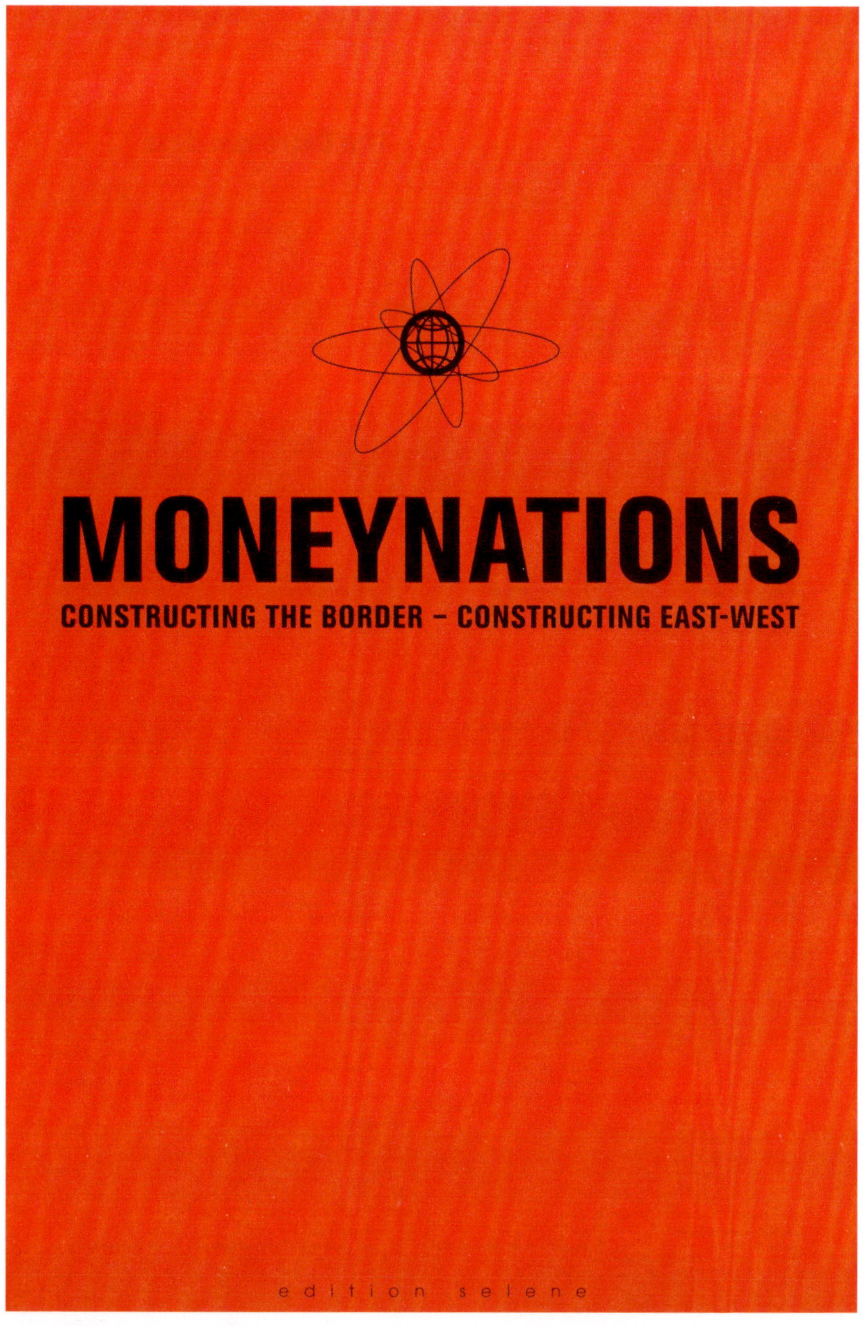




Cover and content page of the publication *MONEYNATIONS: Constructing the Border – Constructing East-West*, edited by Marion von Osten and published by Edition Selene, Vienna, 2003

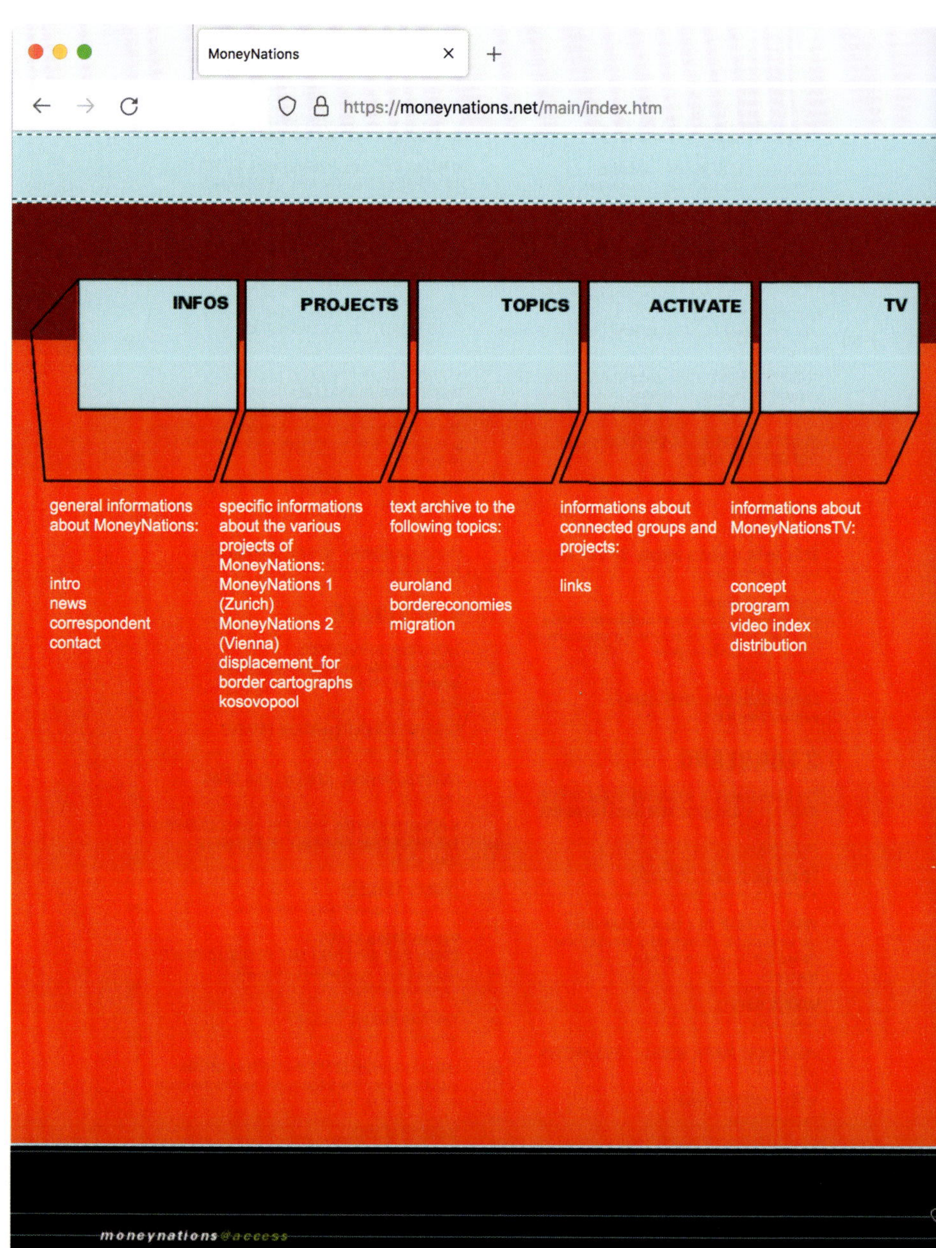


The website *www.moneynations.net*, published in conjunction with the exhibition in Zurich, 1998

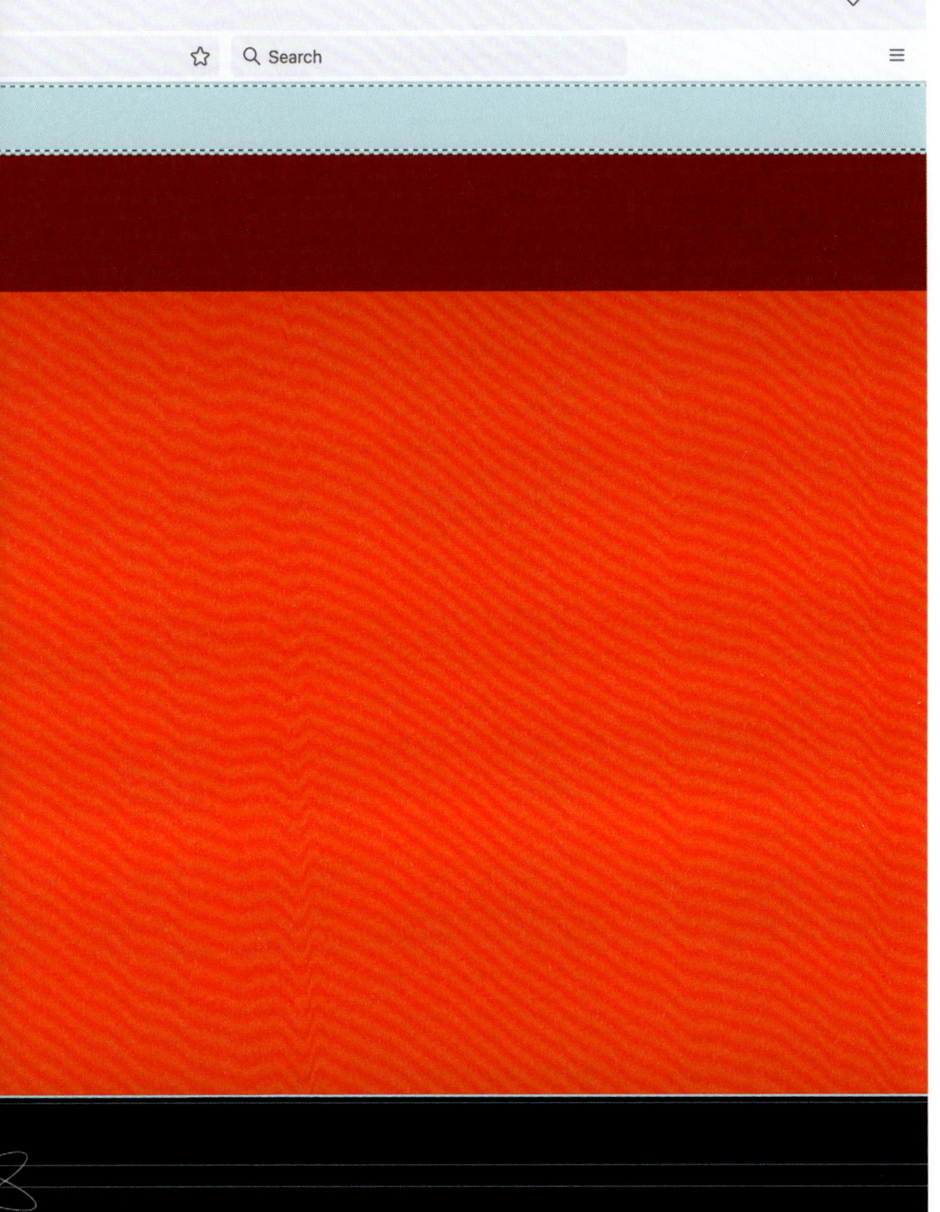

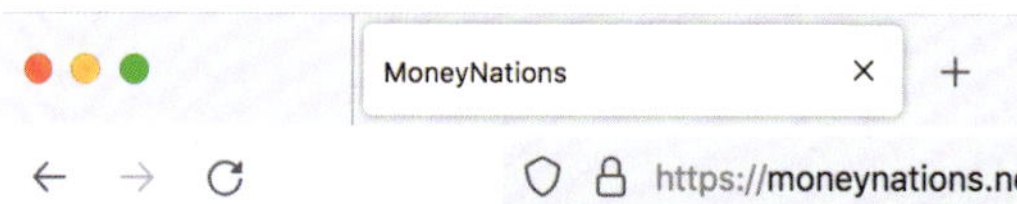




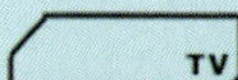


## Join MoneyNations TV with your own video!

You definetly can add new productions to this issues. Please register your video contribution with Marion von Osten marionvonosten@gmx.ch. We offer to copy the videos and, according to the arrangements made with the producers, to produce topical samplers or compile small archives, which again will be distirbuted and sent to the other producers. Renting or copying arrangements must be discussed with the producers in order to make sure that ordered tapes are in fact available when necessary for an event.

We suggest the use of the following topic categorisation for the videos:
1. Border economies.
2. Construction of the "other"; construction of the "East".
3. Changing topographies (State policy;internalsecurity,InnerCityissues).
4. No Neo&endash;Liberalism.
5. Globalisation from below (including examples that point further than Eastern Europe, Migrant initiatives, anti&endash;racism and resistance)

[ announce ]

## MoneyNations TV Edition 1: order the samplers

A first edition of three tapes is already compiled. You can order the samplers for 100 Sfr. each tape. The money goes to the producers!

### 1

**Globalisation-Tape**

"Changing social identies in globalizing cities /Gülsün Karamustafa / Ayse Öncü, VHS15 min, '98

"Money ?" / Marion v. Osten/ Natalie Seitz VHS, 3min, '98

"Kültür" / Ursula Biemann / VHS 8 min, '97

### 2

**Inclusion/Exclusion-Tape**

"Deep Europe Visa Departement" / Dokumenta X / Alexander Davic / Branka Davic, Andreas Broeckmann/ Inke Arns/ Rasa Smite/ Marian Kokot/ Iliana Nedkova/ Eoli Muka/ Tom Bass/ Dimitri Pilkin / Luchezar Boyadjiev. VHS, 10 min, '97

"Project Slovenia /Ljubljana" / Martine Anderfuhren in

### 3

**Border-Tape**

"Borderless Holidays" / Natalie Seitz / Markus Jans VHS 20min

"A-Clips", InnenStadtAktionen 98, Berlin, VHS

"Kosovo a View Inside" /Mediaproject Pristina/ 45 min, VHS, 1997

"Juristische Körper " / dogfilm/



The website *www.moneynations.net*, published in conjunction with the exhibition in Zurich, 1998

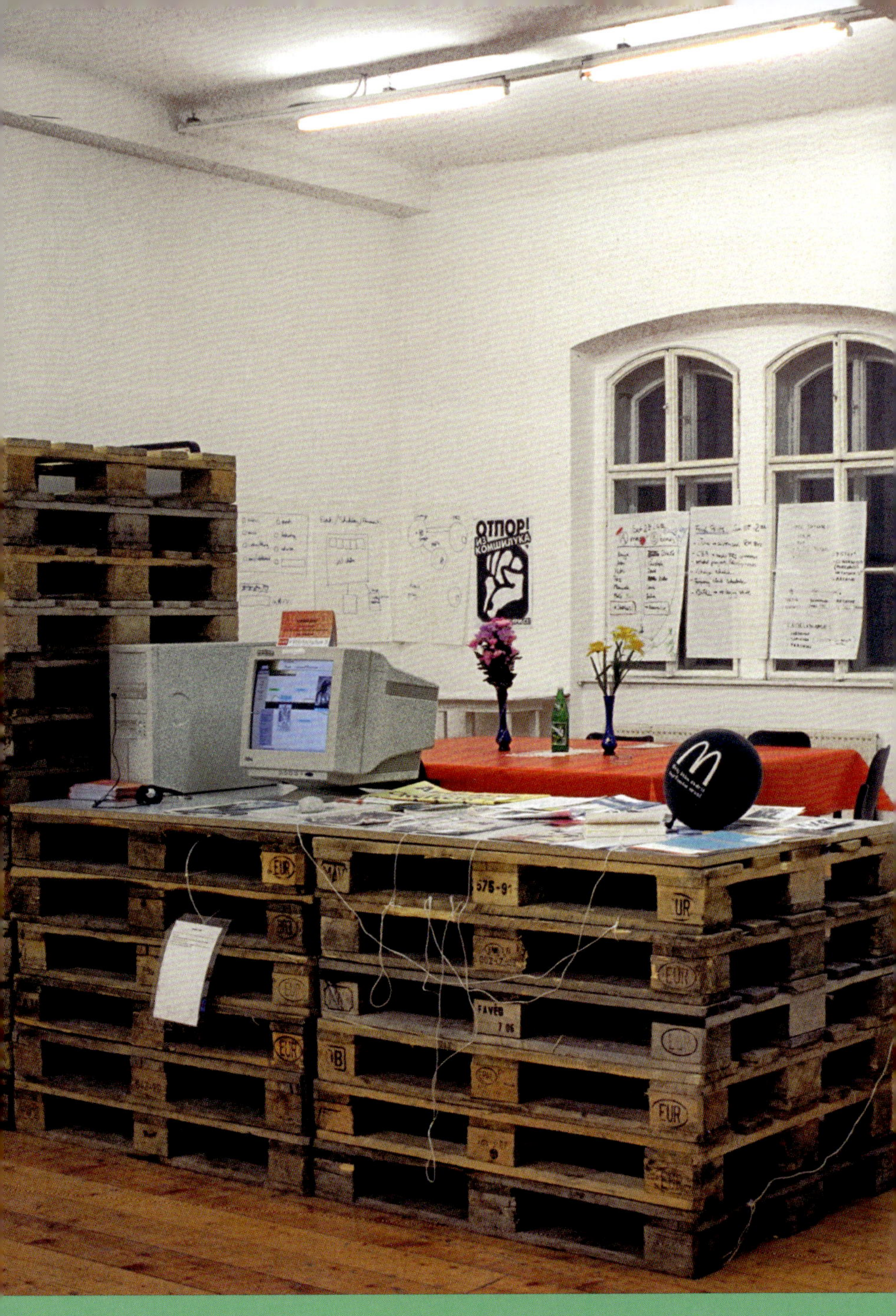

*MoneyNations2*, installation view, Kunsthalle Exnergasse, Vienna, 2001

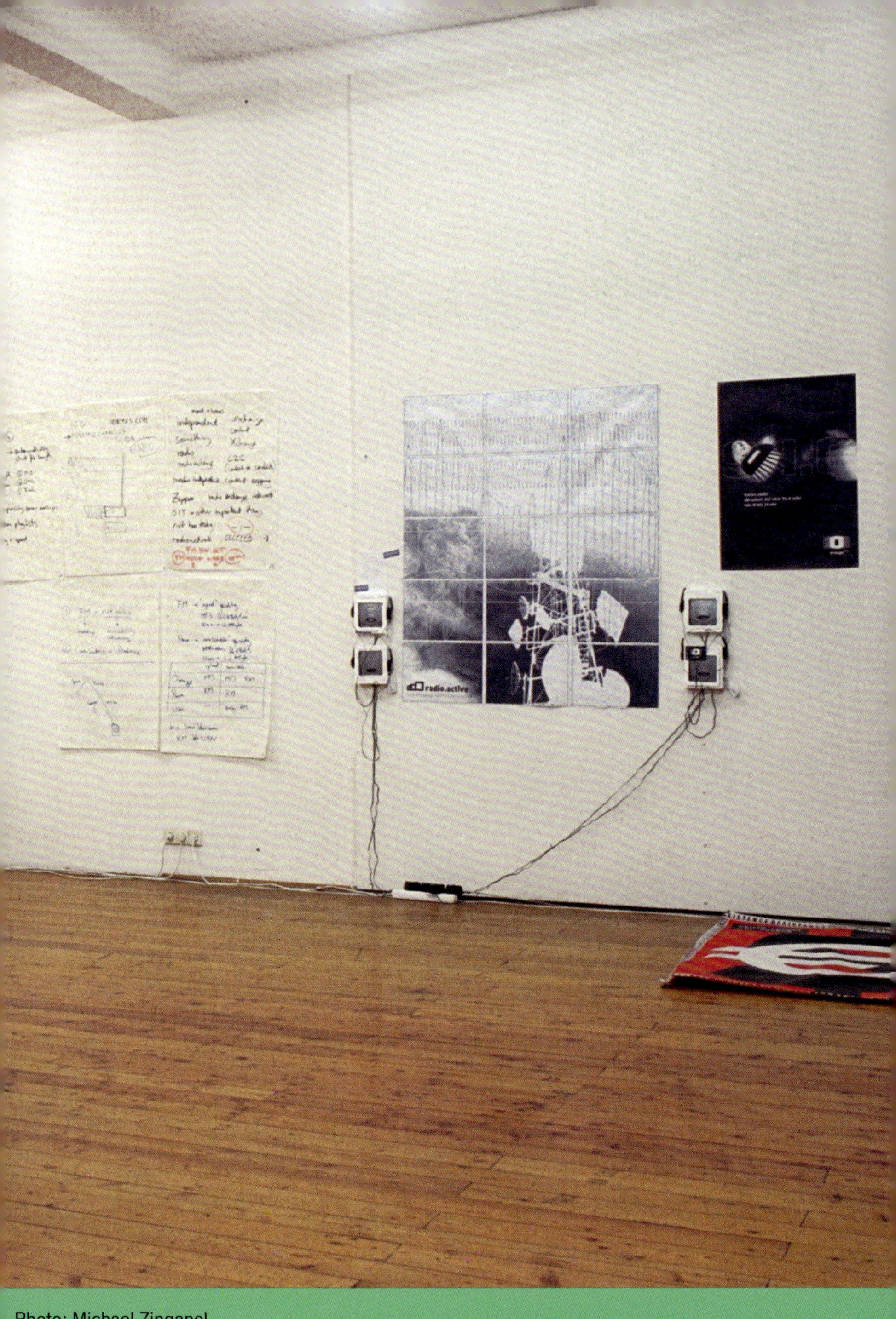



Photo: Michael Zinganel
Source: CPKC, Berlin

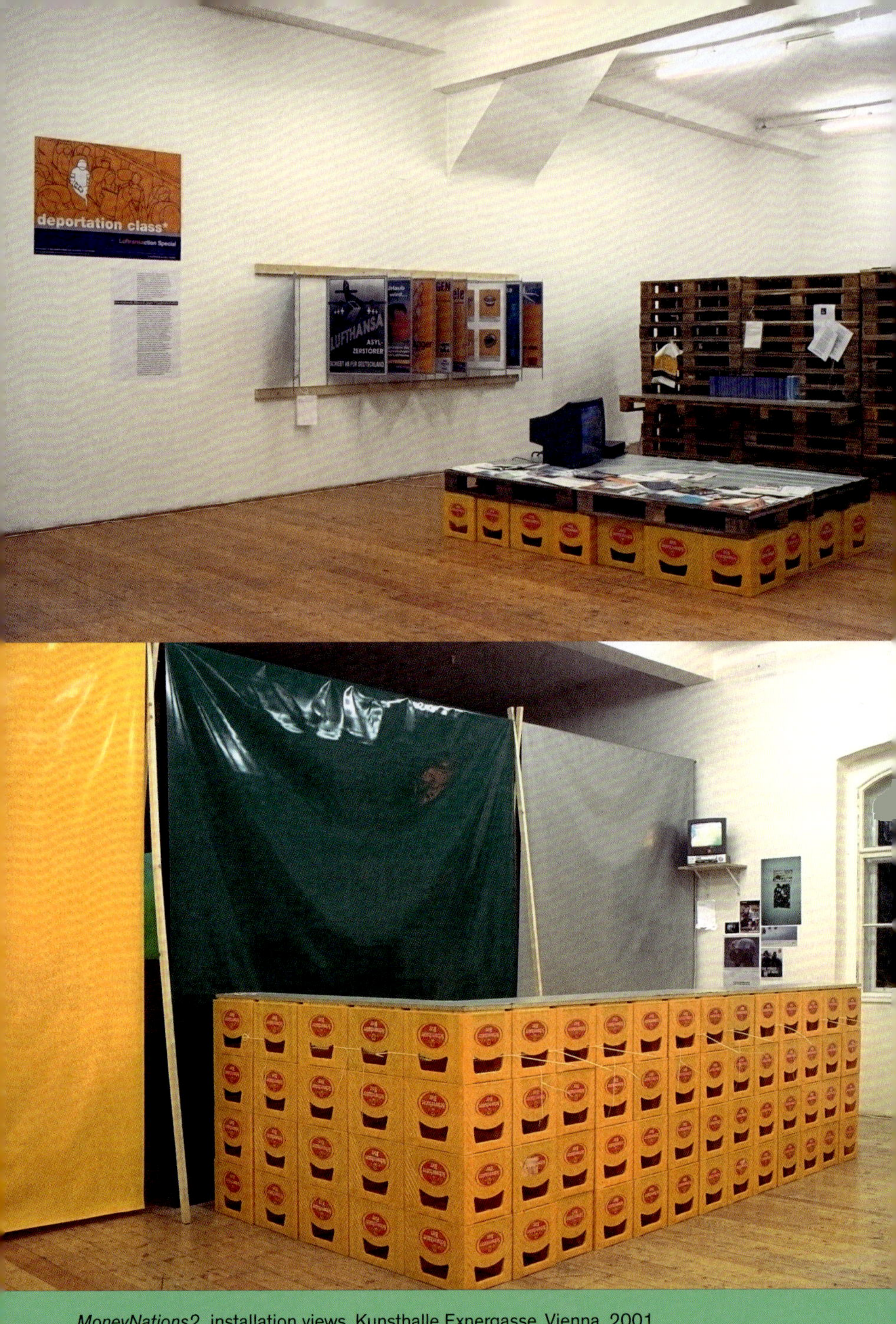

*MoneyNations2*, installation views, Kunsthalle Exnergasse, Vienna, 2001

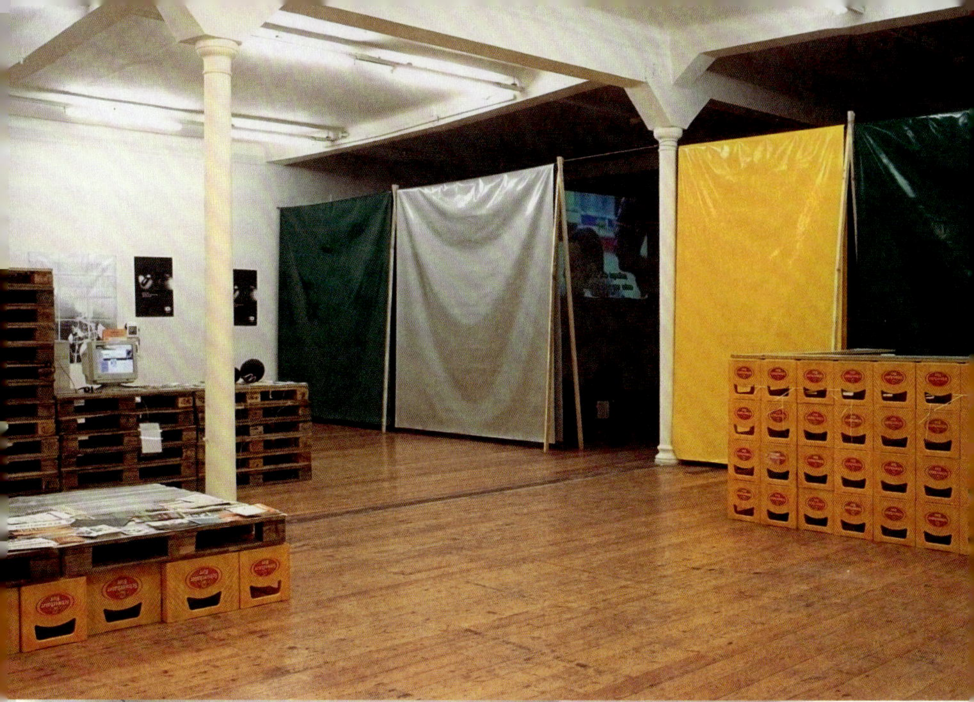

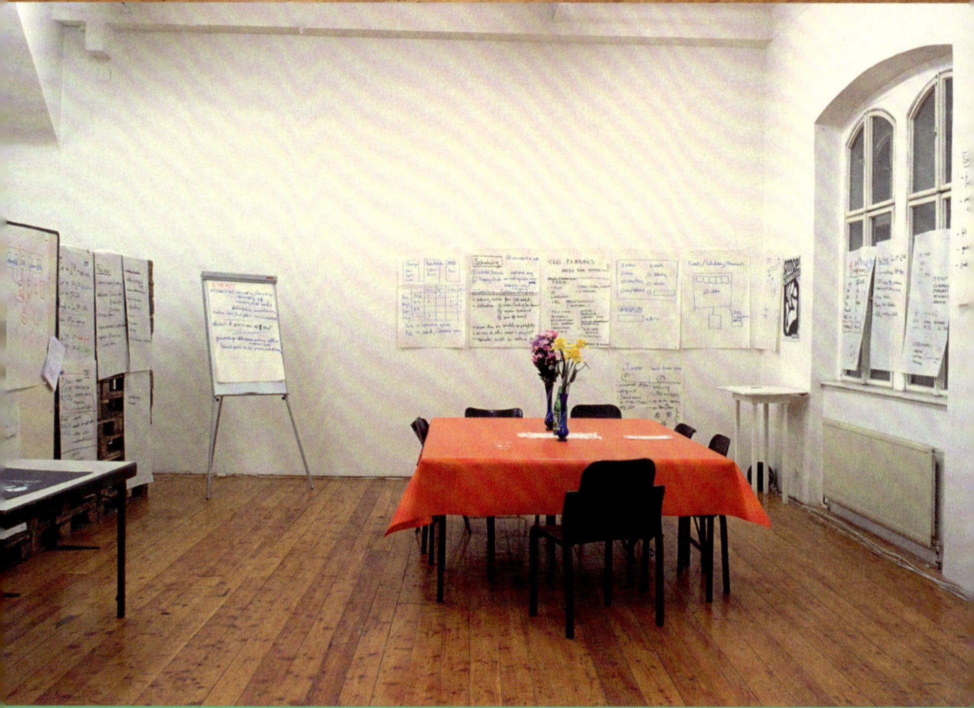

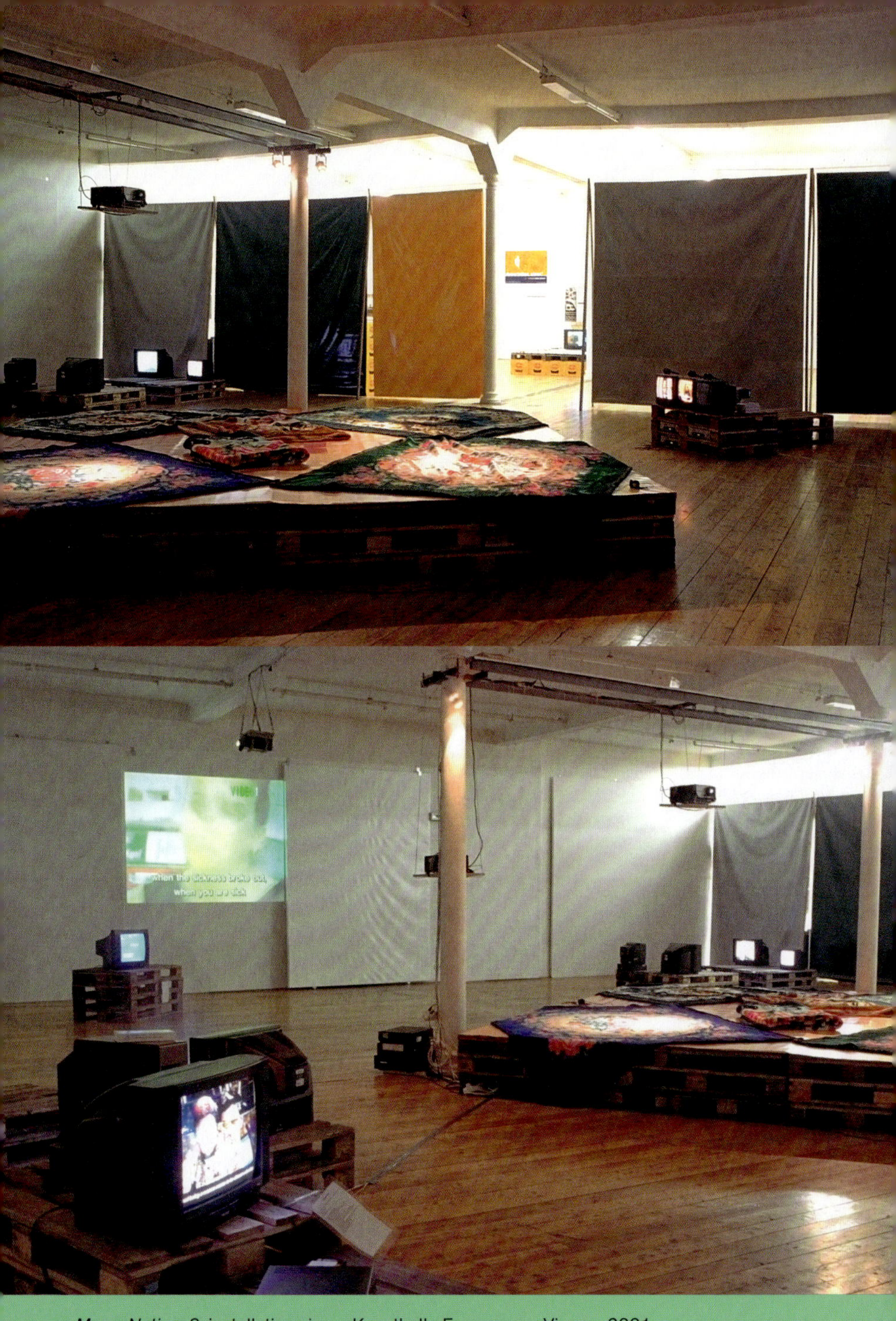

*MoneyNations2*, installation views, Kunsthalle Exnergasse, Vienna, 2001

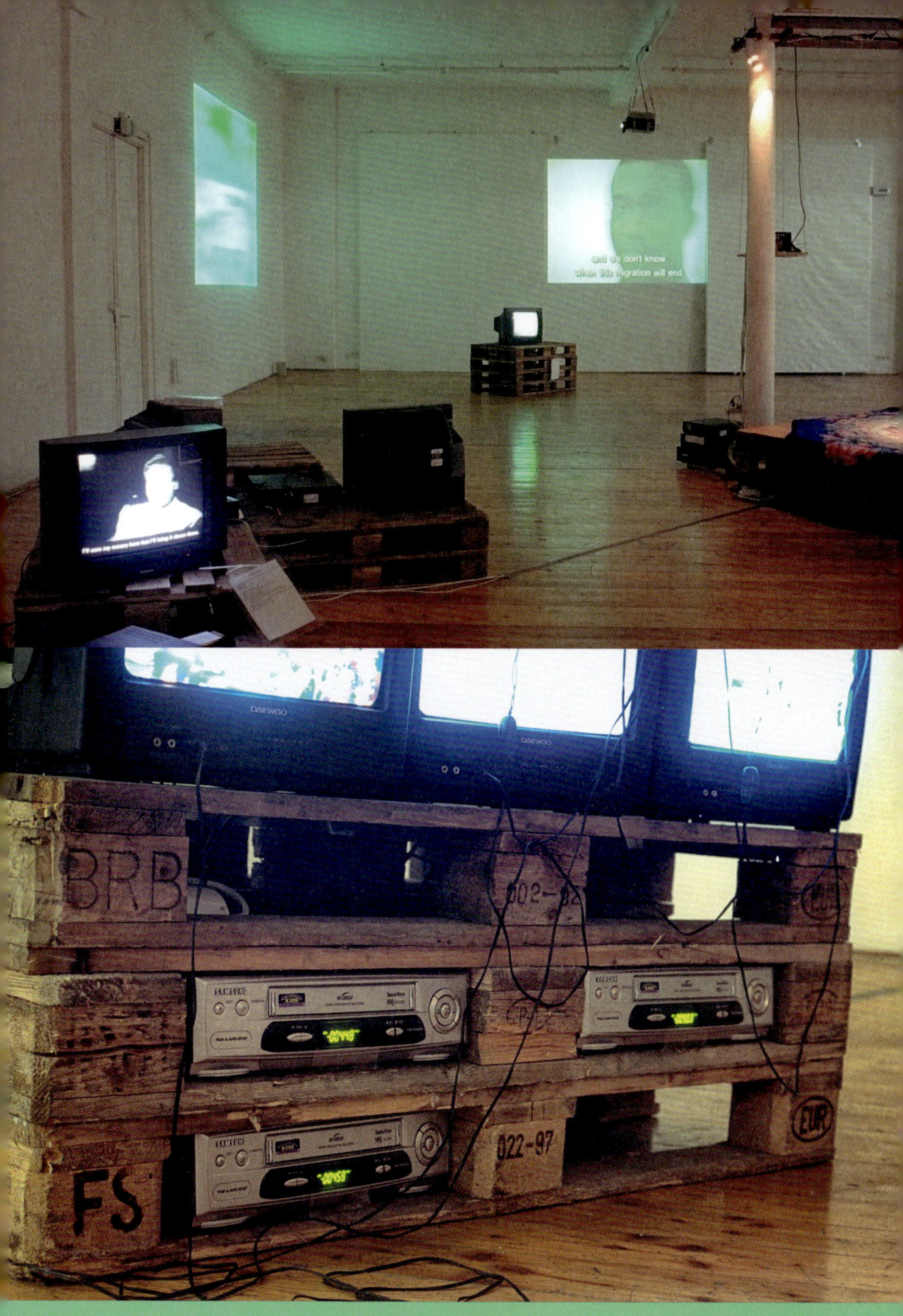



Photos: Michael Zinganel
Source: CPKC, Berlin

*MoneyNations Inventory*
Participants, conferences, lectures,
publications, workshops, exhibitions

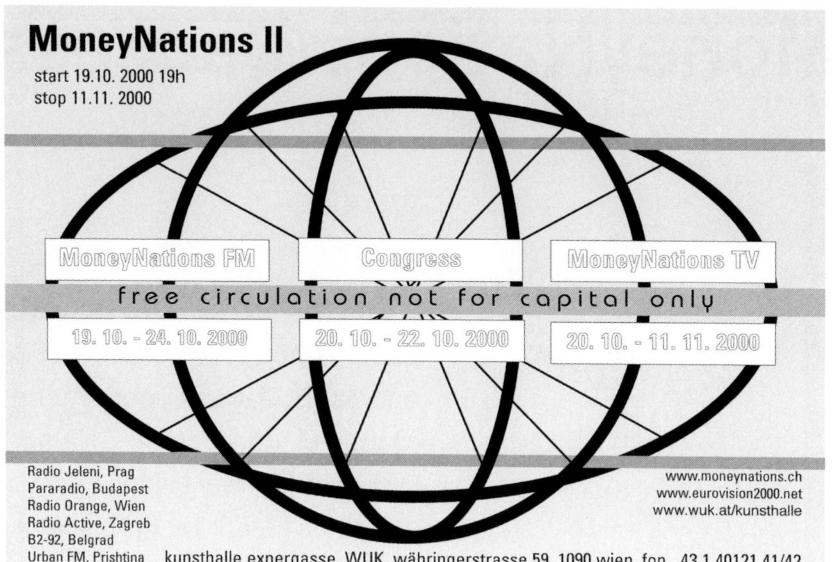

MoneyNations II
start 19.10. 2000 19h
stop 11.11. 2000
MoneyNations FM
Congress
MoneyNations TV
free circulation not for capital only
19. 10. - 24. 10. 2000
20. 10. - 22. 10. 2000
20. 10. - 11. 11. 2000
Radio Jeleni, Prag
Pararadio, Budapest
Radio Orange, Wien
Radio Active, Zagreb
B2-92, Belgrad
Urban FM, Prishtina
www.moneynations.ch
www.eurovision2000.net
www.wuk.at/kunsthalle
kunsthalle exnergasse, WUK, währingerstrasse 59, 1090 wien, fon _43 1 40121 41/42

# MoneyNations@access

**Participants**

A-Clip (Berlin), Apsolutno (Novi Sad), Mehmet Akiol (Zurich), Edit András (Budapest), Joerg Arendt (Bonn), Marion Baruch / Name Diffusion (Paris / Milan), Paola di Bello / Marco Biraghi (Milan), Jochen Becker (Berlin), Marica Bender / RadioZid (Sarajevo), Luchezar Boyadjiev (Sofia), Iara Boubnova (Sofia), Fritz Burschel / kein mensch ist illegal, Jana Cvikova / ASPEKT (Bratislava), Eva Danzl Suarez / FIZ (Zurich), Dogfilm (Berlin), Melita Gabric /

Concept:
Marion von Osten

Webdesign & newspaper layout:
Natalie Seitz


The information on page 74–87 was gathered from the publications *The Correspondent* and *MONEYNATIONS,* the website *www.moneynations.net* and through conversations with Peter Spillmann

# (Zurich, 1998)

Shedhalle, Rote Fabrik, P.O.Box, Seestrasse 395, 8038 Zurich

Blaz Habjan / Martine Anderfuhren (Ljubljana / Geneva), Hex TV (Cologne), Berta Jottar (New York), k3000 (Zurich), Gülsün Karamustafa (Istanbul), Beat Leuthardt (Basel), Level Ltd. (Zurich), Geert Lovink (Amsterdam), Medienhilfe Ex-Jugoslavien (Zurich), Marton Oblath (Budapest), Ayşe Öncü (Istanbul), Marion von Osten (Berlin / Zurich), Drazen Pantic / B92 (Belgrade), Marko Peljhan / Ljudmila (Ljubljana), Lia & Dan Perjovschi (Bucharest), Pascal Petignat / Peter Riedlinger (Zurich / Vienna), Sascha Roesler (Zurich), Polnischer Sozialrat (Berlin), Kalin Serapionov (Sofia), Oliver Sertic / ATTACK! (Zagreb), Natalie Seitz / Markus Jans (Lucerne), Nedko Solakow (Sofia), Peter Spillmann (Zurich), Deep Europe / V2_East-Syndicate, Mina Vuletic / B92 (Belgrade), Anna Wessely (Budapest), Jeta Xharra / Media Project (Pristina), Želimir Žilnik / Terra Film (Novi Sad).

Organisation / proofreading / editors:
Agnes Bieber, Marion v. Osten, Natalie Seitz, Sascha Roesler

Translations & English proofreading:
Gabriela Meier

Conference:
*Border Economies*

Name Diffusion

Luchezar Boyadjiev

Lia Perjovschi

Gülsün Karamustafa

Jochen Becker

Peter Riedlinger &
Pascal Petignat

kein mensch ist illegal

Polnischer Sozialrat

23.10 – 25.10. 1998

The congress was divided into three days. It revolved around the economic background of the "sibling pair" racism / sexism. These power and inequality relations were linked in relation to the massive expansion of the EU borders and their significance for new forms of exploitation in Eastern Europe.

*MoneyNations TV*

*MoneyNations TV* was an open video exchange project between Middle, Central and Southeastern European producers in the framework of *MoneyNations*.

Publication

*The Correspondent*

This workshop was organized in the framework of the *MoneyNations@access* project in cooperation with Medienhilfe Ex-Jugoslawien, Labor k3000 and radio-producers Level Ltd. (Zurich). The workshop took place from 27 to 31 Oct. 1998. Starting at 2 p.m. each day in the premises of Labor k3000, the workshop aimed at joint productions of radio programs and videos.

## Lectures

1998     *MoneyNations*, Kulturelle Arbeit im Zeitalter der Globalisierung, Osteuropakongress, ifa Gallerie, Stuttgart und Liget Gallery, Budapest

1999     „Strategien der Selbstorganisation", die Projekte *MoneyNations* und k3000, Biennale Venedig, im Rahmen von Oreste Space

**Friday, October 23rd, 1998**

Beat Leuthardt, author of *Festung Europa* (Fortress Europe), will present the confused relationship between private economy (Siemens) and the strengthening of border security in so-called transit countries (Latvia, Ukraine, Poland).

The campaign *kein mensch ist illegal* (no one is illegal) will be presented. This campaign started on the occasion of Documenta X (Kassel, Germany) and is run by an anti-racist group together with cultural workers.

Lecture about the Border Workshops and activist artistic practice against U.S. border policy by American / Mexican artist Berta Jottar.

Final discussion about border creation and resistance.

**Saturday, October 24th, 1998**

The Calida Story: Mehmet Akiol, GBI (Swiss Union for Construction and Industry) will talk about the battles of workers in the Swiss textile industry. Bettina Musiolek (not confirmed) will talk about companies out-sourced to Southeastern Europe.

Eva Danzel Suarez of the Frauen-informationszentrum Zürich (Women's Information Center) will discuss trade in women in the context of asylum-seekers' legislation and economy. The following discussion aims to investigate what we should be demanding as a result of this situation.

Suitcase Trade: Dr. Anna Wessely and Marton Oblath, sociologists from Budapest, will present the research project *Shopping Tourism*, which had been investigated by various scientists from Central Europe in order to create a new system to evaluate border trades

*Die Polen vom Potsdamer Platz* (The Polish from Potsdam Square): A film about the life of Polish commuting workers in Berlin

**Sunday, October 25th, 1998**

Talking Absolute Business: Peter Spillmann (k3000 Zurich) will present his research into the Eastern European Fund and its effects on transnational wealth accumulation.

Globalisation from Below?: Geert Lovink, media activist and political scientist from Amsterdam, will discuss the function of stock market speculator George Soros in conjunction with NGOs and civil society in Central and Southeastern Europe.

ASPEKT: A feminist magazine project from Bratislava, Slovakia, will present itself. The focus will be on the position of an independent institution within the framework of the current economic / social situation in Eastern Europe

RADEK: An art magazine from Moscow will be presented by Oleg Kireev. RADEK's editing cooperative sees itself as an activist group. Which approaches to practice, politics and art are adopted by this independent institution?

Final discussion about inclusion and exclusion of Eastern European positions in the international art market with Luchezar Boyadiev (artist, Sofia), Iara Boubnova (curator, Sofia / Moscow), Edit András (art historian, Budapest), Oleg Kireev (art critic, Moscow), and including the audience. Facilitation: Marion v. Osten (Shedhalle).

# MoneyNations 2



Mogniss Abdallah (Paris), Dragan Ambrosic (Belgrade), Zeigam Azizov (London), awareness (Vienna), Jochen Becker (Berlin), Manuela Bojadzijev (Frankfurt / M.), bordercartograph / name diffusion (Paris), B2-92 (Belgrade), Anna Daucíková (Bratislava), dérive (Vienna), Die Bunte Zeitung (Vienna), Helmut Dietrich (Berlin), Dana Diminescu (Paris / RU), Deportation Class (kein mensch ist illegal), DocVideo (Turin), Echo / Simone Bader, Anna Kowalska, Martin Krenn (Vienna), female sequences (Vienna), fewor (Vienna),

Exhibiton:
Peter Spillmann, Marion von Osten

Conference:
Jochen Becker, Marion von Osten, Gabriele Marth, Jo Schmeiser

# (Vienna, 2000)

Kunsthalle Exnergasse, Währinger Straße 59, 1090 Vienna

Micz Flor (Berlin), Jesko Fezer (Berlin), get to attack (Vienna), Encarnación Gutiérrez Rodríguez (Hanover / Frankfurt), Brian Holmes (Paris), Kanak Attak, Gülsün Karamustafa (Istanbul), LEFÖ (Vienna), MAIZ (Vienna), malmoe (Vienna), Gabriele Marth (Vienna), MUND (Vienna), nylon (Vienna), Marion von Osten (Berlin / Zurich), PEREGRINA (Vienna), Susanna Perin (Zurich / Rome), Radio Active (Zagreb), Radio FRO (Linz), Radio Orange (Vienna), Roma 2000 / Andreas Lehner, u.a. (Oberwart), Pararadio (Budapest), Jenny Perlin (New York), Jayce Salloum (Vancouver), Jo Schmeiser (Vienna), Peter Spillmann (Zurich), Mark Saunders (London), Sava Tatic (Prague), Staatsarchitektur / Klub Zwei (Vienna), stimme (Vienna), TATblatt (Vienna), Katalin Timar (Budapest), Urban FM (Pristina), Angie Waller (New York), Anna Wessely (Budapest), Marion West (Hamburg), Netzwerk V2 / East_Syndicate; der Forschungsgemeinschaft Flucht und Migration, Polnischer Sozialrat Berlin, kein mensch ist illegal

Grafic and web design:
Natalie Seitz, Peter Spillmann, Marion von Osten

Kunsthalle Exnergasse:
Franziska Kasper, Andrea Löbel

Architecture:
Michael Zinganel, Ernst Muck

# Exhibition

## Video Works

- *New Borders*, Jenny Perlin, VHS 22 New York, 2000
- *EUrope on your doorstep*, VHS 20, Micz Flor, Berlin, 2000
- *Everything And Nothing*, Jayce Salloum, Vancouver, video installation, 2000
- *Loading Animated*, Angie Waller, VHS 10 New York, 2000
- *Fashion Is Work,* Karamustafa / v. Osten / Spillmann, video installation, Istanbul / Zurich 1999
- *Migrasophia*, Zeigam Azizov, VHS 8, London, 2000
- *Beyond The Fencing*, Susanna Perin, VHS 12, Zurich / Rome, 2000
- *And This Wind Hurts*, DocVideo, VHS 45, Turin
- *The Truth Lies In Rostock*, spectacle / Mark Saunders, VHS 78, London 1993
- *Staatsarchitektur, Klub Zwei*, 1997 / 1998, VHS 105', Vienna; (*Ohneland* Hatice Ayten, 1995 / *StaatsPersonal Teil 1*, Klub Zwei, 1997 / *Gekommen bin ich der Arbeit wegen*, Goran Rebic, 1987 / *Gülüzar*, Hatice Ayten, 1994 / *StaatsPersonal Teil 2*, Klub Zwei, 1997 / Material from *Achtung Staatsgrenze*, Sabine Derflinger / Bernhard Pötscher, 1996 / StaatsPersonal Teil 3, Klub Zwei, 1997 / *Land des Lächelns*, Hito Steyerl, 1996 / *StaatsPersonal Teil 4*, Klub Zwei, 1997)
- *Douce France*, Mogniss Abdallah & Ken Fero , VHS, 52, Paris 1992 *nordreise*, Marion von Osten & R.R.I.O. Sans Papier Office, VHS 30, Antwerpen / Zurich 2000
- *Macht und Gehorsam–Schule unterrichtet*, Martin Krenn in cooperation with Paul Leitner, Nina Mangel, Quilla Mederos, Niki Voraberger, Lisi Ziegelmaier, VHS 23', Vienna, 1998 / STRUKTURELLE GEWALT-as well as talks and images by Dani Busic, Djonia, Oliveira Mendes, Anna Kowalska, Simone Bader, VHS, 25", Vienna 1999 / 2000

## Entrance Area / Archives

- Deportation Class (kein mensch ist illegal, Cologne), presentation of campaign posters from the Campaign against Deportation and Airport Regulation (www.deportation-alliance.com)
- *Roma 2000* (Oberwart), electronic cultural documentation on the history and the situation of Romas in Burgenland and Austria
- *Drill Instructor. Captain Full Metal Jack*, Jochen Becker / Jesko Fezer, video / installation, Berlin 1997 / 2000

The conference covers a wide range of issues from postcolonial critique, anti-racist work and network activism to cultural production.

## MoneyNations FM

Participants:

Radio Orange
(Eva Egermann, Pez; Vienna)

Radio FRO
(Alexander Baratsits,
Manuela Mittermayer; Linz)

B92
(Robert Klajn; Belgrade)

Pararadio
(Peter Notari; Budapest)

Radio Active
(Zeljko Blace, Vanja Nicolic; Zagreb)

Radio Jeleni
(Derek Holzer; Prague)

Urban FM
(Atdhe Mulla; Pristina)

Radio 21
(Jeta Xharra; London)

## MoneyNations TV

With clips by A-Clip (Berlin), Martine Anderfuhren (Geneva), Jörg Arendt (Bonn), Ursula Biemann (Zurich), Paula di Bello / Marco Biraghi (Milan), Deep Europe / V2_East-Syndicate, Dogfilm (Berlin), HexTV (Cologne), Gülsün Karamustafa (Istanbul), Marion von Osten (Berlin / Zurich), Natalie Seitz (Zurich), Peter Spillmann (Zurich)

**Friday, October 20st, 2000**

<u>Europe and the Refugees
Borderlines</u>

Helmut Dietrich,
Forschungsgesellschaft Flucht und
Migration (Research society refuge
and migration), Berlin

Settlement in the mobility, Dana
Diminescu, currently researching at
Maison des sciences de l'homme, Paris
and is chief coordinator of the research
project *Les circulations migratoires*

Discrimination against Romas in
Hungary, Anna Wessely, sociologist and
art historian, ELTE University, Budapest

Romas in Austria: on the exhibition
*Roma 2000*, Andreas Lehner, curator
of *Roma 2000*, Markt Allhau, Emmerich
Gärtner-Horvath, Volkshochschule der
Burgenländischen Roma, Oberwart

<u>History of resistance</u>

Douce France / Sweet France:
documentary film by Mogniss Abdallah
& Ken Fero (60', 1992)

**Saturday, October 21st, 2000**

<u>Resistance Politics</u>

The Beur Movement. A (hi)story of resistance. Mogniss Abdallah, Agence IM'media (LÎagence de l'immigration et des cultures urbaines) Paris, Manuela Bojadžijev (Kanak Attak, Frankfurt / M)

<u>Anti-racism Politics: Strategies for Public Relations</u>

Deportation Class (kein mensch ist illegal): presentation of the activist alliance and its campaign against deportation and airport regulations, Munich / Cologne

fewor–plattform für eine welt ohne rassismus (platform for a world without racism), Vienna

MAIZ Autonomes Zentrum von und für Migrantinnen (Autonomes Center by and for Migrant Women), Linz

PEREGRINA Beratungsstelle für ausländische Frauen (Counselling Center for foreign Women), Vienna

LEFÖ Lateinamerikanische Emigrierte Frauen in Österreich (Latin American Women Emigrants in Austria), Vienna

Feministischer Widerstandsrat (Feminist Resistance Council), Vienna (requested)

<u>Art in Practice</u>

*bordercartograph*: Presentation of the webpage, a communication project between France and Africa, Marion Baruch, artist, Paris. www.moneynations.ch/cartograph

Look back / look forward: Reflection on a seminar project on the social space of migration at the International Women's University in Hanover, Gülsün Karamustafa, artist, Istanbul

Power and obedience / structural violence: students from the school at WUK and 2nd generation youth with Simone Bader, Anna Kowalska, Martin Krenn, Dani Busic (requested), Djonia Oliveira Mendes (requested), Phillipp Winkler (requested), artists and students, Vienna

get to attack, Vienna: presentation of the Viennese Resistance Alliance with representatives from get to attack, Vienna

<u>Political Geography</u>

Cross the Border: Imaginary Maps, Global Solidarities, Brian Holmes, (ne pas plier), cultural critic and translator, Paris

**Sunday, October 22nd, 2000**

<u>State Architechture and Gender I</u>

Workshop with: Manuela Bojadzijev
(Kanak Attak, Frankfurt / M), Gabriele
Marth und Jo Schmeiser (Vor der
Information, feminist magazine for
art, film, politics and theory / Vienna),
Marion West, activist, Hamburg

<u>State Architechture and Gender II</u>

Parallel Activities: on gay / lesbian
movements in Slovakia, Anna Daučíková
(Initiative Anders), artist / university
lecturer, Bratislava

Ethics and Visuality Workshop: Katalin
Timar, art historian / curator, Budapest,
provides information on experiences
involving political positions within
the field of art history.

For feminist, anti-racism action beyond
identity politics. Encarnación Gutiérrez
Rodríguez, cultural studies scholar,
Hannover / Frankfurt

<u>Media Practice and Campaign Politics</u>

The significance of youth and fanzine
culture for the resistance movement
in Serbia: Dragan Ambrosic, Belgrad

Alternative media strategies and
objectives of *MoneyNations.FM*, Sava
Tatic, theorist, Prague

<u>Media Practice and Campagne Politics II</u>

Discussion on campaigns and media
that aim to combat racist and sexist
(state) politics in Austria

With representatives from:
awareness!–the african voice in europe
(requested)

dérive–Zeitschrift für Stadtforschung
(magazine for urban research)

Die Bunte Zeitung–Zeitschrift von
MigrantInnen aus allen Kontinenten
(magazine by migrants from all
continents)

female sequences–Frauen Lesben
Kultur Heft (womensâ lesbiansâ cultural
paper)

MUND–Medien Unabhängiger
Nachrichten Dienst (independent
media news service)

malmoe–ein neues Zeitungsprojekt
(a new magazine project)

nylon–KunstStoff zu Feminismus
und Popkultur (artificial material on
feminism and pop culture)

stimme. von und für minderheiten
(voice. from and for minorities)

TATblatt–antirassistische Zeitschrift
(anti-racist magazine) (requested)

*Going Sideways*
A conversation between the editors and
Divided Publishing, KUNCI and Rab-Rab Press

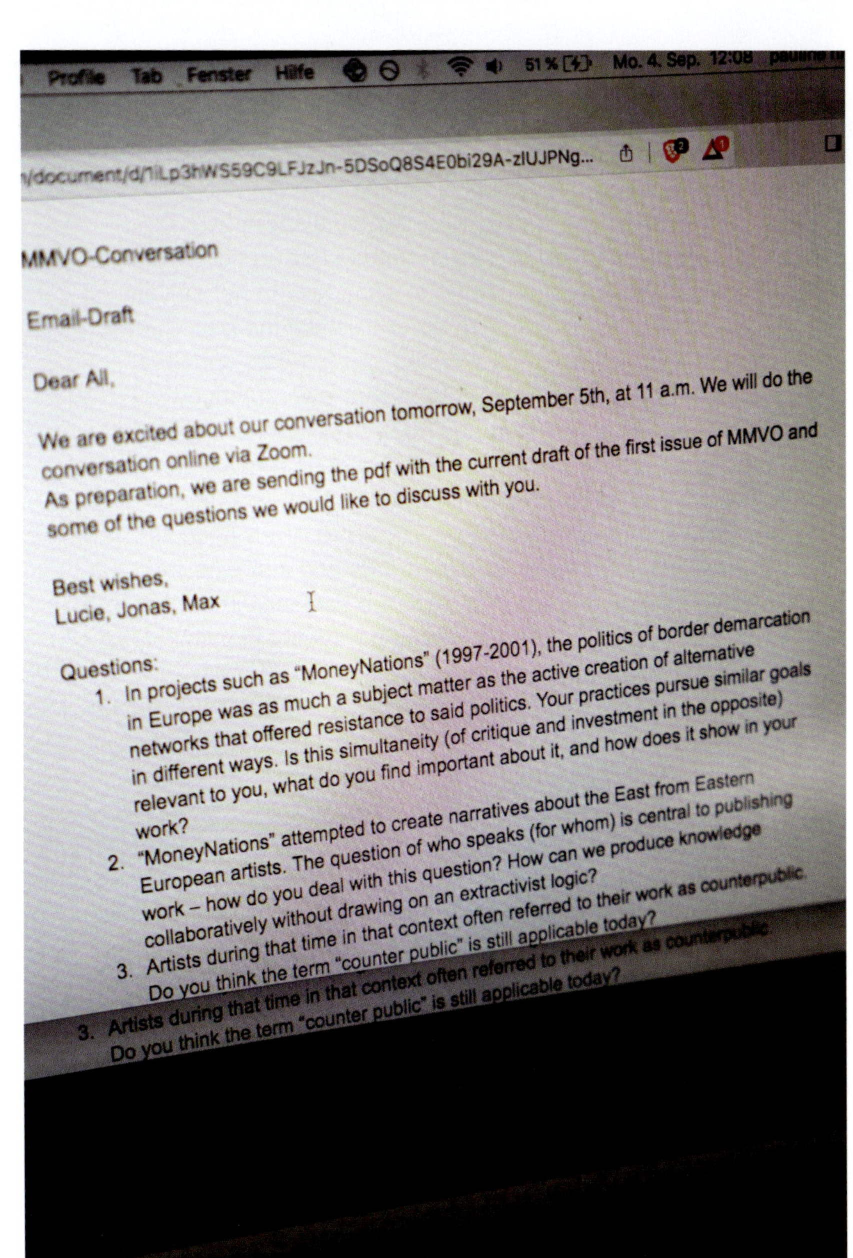



/document/d/1iLp3hWS59C9LFJzJn-5DSoQ8S4E0bi29A-zIUJPNg...

MMVO-Conversation

Email-Draft

Dear All,

We are excited about our conversation tomorrow, September 5th, at 11 a.m. We will do the conversation online via Zoom.
As preparation, we are sending the pdf with the current draft of the first issue of MMVO and some of the questions we would like to discuss with you.

Best wishes,
Lucie, Jonas, Max

Questions:
1. In projects such as "MoneyNations" (1997-2001), the politics of border demarcation in Europe was as much a subject matter as the active creation of alternative networks that offered resistance to said politics. Your practices pursue similar goals in different ways. Is this simultaneity (of critique and investment in the opposite) relevant to you, what do you find important about it, and how does it show in your work?
2. "MoneyNations" attempted to create narratives about the East from Eastern European artists. The question of who speaks (for whom) is central to publishing work – how do you deal with this question? How can we produce knowledge collaboratively without drawing on an extractivist logic?
3. Artists during that time in that context often referred to their work as counterpublic. Do you think the term "counter public" is still applicable today?
3. Artists during that time in that context often referred to their work as counterpublic. Do you think the term "counter public" is still applicable today?

**Jonas (MMVO):**
Thank you everyone for joining this conversation. Starting with
this edition of the project *MoneyNations*, we are going to
publish material from the archive of the artist, curator and
researcher Marion von Osten, who passed away in 2020.
With this publishing series we aim to map her practice through
her projects, and, more generally, to engage with her specific
artistic and political methods in order to make them productive
for the present. That's why we invited you to relate and react
to her archival material, in relation to your own practices.
The first publication in the series deals, as I mentioned,
with the project *MoneyNations*, which materialized as two
exhibitions—one at Shedhalle in Zurich in 1998 and the other
at Kunsthalle Exnergasse in Vienna in 2000. Many aspects
of *MoneyNations* led to specific methods and interests she
developed further in other contexts. You can see similar forms
of network-building between cultural producers in many of the
projects that followed, such as *Atelier Europa* at Kunstverein
Munich in 2004, *Projekt Migration* in Cologne (2002–2006), or
*bauhaus imaginista* (2017–2019). One can also trace discursive
connections to, for example, the project *Former West* (2014–
2016) to which Marion contributed.

**Lucie (MMVO):**
The series is also an attempt to be in conversation with Marion;
we feel an urge to build on her decentralizing, collectivist
approaches, something Jonas and I experienced when working
with her in different contexts. So, for us this is also a series
of conversations, which led us to initiate this format as a way
of expanding it to other voices, and we are curious to hear
how your practices might tie to methodologies developed
in *MoneyNations*.
*MoneyNations* dealt with border demarcations and border
policies in Europe after 1989, and it's interesting to see how
the project takes border politics as a subject matter while at the

same time, on an infrastructural level, working actively towards creating decentralized networks that oppose those very politics. It's this simultaneity, among other things, that we'd like to talk about with all of you. Max, do you want to add something to the overall series or to this first issue in particular?

**Max (MMVO):**
A quick note regarding the status of the documents we are publishing in this volume. Most of the material we're working with is sourced from Marion's estate, which is located in Berlin. It is housed at Peter Spillmann's residence, who was her partner and long-term collaborator and he also played an important role in *MoneyNations*. It's our primary source, which is in the process of becoming a publicly accessible archive.

**Lucie:**
Let's start with a brief introduction round. I can start. I'm a researcher based in Basel, working at the Critical Media Lab, focusing on critical publishing strategies. I'm part of this series MMVO together with Max and Jonas.

**Jonas:**
I'm Jonas; I run Wirklichkeit Books, and I currently also run the archive of the Kunstverein Munich. That's why I'm dividing my time between Berlin and Munich at the moment.

**Max:**
I'm Max Stocklosa, and I'm an artist. I am currently involved in building Marion's archive here in Berlin together with Peter Spillmann.

**Eleanor (Divided Publishing):**
I'm Eleanor. I have an art and theory background, and with Camilla, I am co-publisher of Divided.

**Camilla (Divided Publishing):**

I'm Camilla. I'm the other half of Divided. We publish books.

**Ferdi (KUNCI Study Forum & Collective):**

I'm Ferdi. I'm currently based in Berlin. I'm part of a collective called KUNCI Study Forum & Collective from Indonesia. But I'm also currently a lecturer in Erlangen. So, I'm commuting between Berlin and Erlangen.

**Sezgin (Rab-Rab Press):**

I am Sezgin, now based in Helsinki, but I'm also quite active in Kosovo, where I'm from; here, I run Rab-Rab Press. Besides Rab-Rab, I'm also involved in other publishing-related projects like OEI magazine in Stockholm and the Pykë-Presje collective in Prizren, Kosovo.

**Camilla:**

I should have also mentioned I'm based in London, and Eleanor is in Brussels. So we work between the two places.

**Eleanor:**

Can I ask how you started this project? What brought you to Marion von Osten?

**Jonas:**

I got to know Marion in 2017, when I started working with her as a research and production assistant in the context of the exhibition project *bauhaus imaginista*. That's how I met Marion and also Peter. When Marion passed away, Peter asked me if I wanted to help him build the archive. Right after my time at *bauhaus imaginista*—and retrospectively, I can say, very much inspired by this experience—I started Wirklichkeit Books. In this context the idea of a publishing series appeared.

**Lucie**:

You initiated the series by inviting Max and me. I have been working with Marion on a research project on micro-organizations, and I have also worked with Peter in Switzerland. We got in touch through a shared interest in continuing some of the discussions we had with Marion.

**Max**:

I never met Marion. In 2021, Jonas and I, together with Johanna Klingler and Verena Buttmann, worked on an exhibition titled *A Cultural Center in Konstanz*, which had as one of its subjects Berlin in the '90s and the politicized art of that time. In this context Marion kept popping up. So, from then on we continuously read her texts and I got more and more interested, and eventually I took over the archive job when Jonas left for Munich.

**Jonas**:

The first question we'd like to ask you addresses the above-mentioned simultaneity in *MoneyNations*, of researching and working together on a subject matter—in this case the border demarcations in Europe after '89—and at the same time the example of investing in alternative networks that offer resistance to set policies. Is the simultaneity of critique and investment in infrastructure relevant to you as well? How does it show in your work? Sezgin, do you want to start?

**Sezgin**:

This is an interesting approach, to pick up one particular trajectory in curating from that specific moment in the '90s, and to contextualize it within this conversation. Instead of a purely academic approach, which is also important, this is opening up other layers. And it resonates with my own engagement with archives. Before responding directly to your question, let me share some impressions. This may be my answer for now. Let's start with the exhibition title,

*MoneyNations*: it is the kind of art exhibition that starts with a thesis, proposing that the concept of the nation is not only about nationalism, that nation and identity are not only related to affectual circumstances, or the psychologization of very complex ideological formations, but is, in fact, related to something as concrete as money. If at the very beginning you locate the idea of a nation as being connected with money, you then have a specific idea of what a nation is—which is that nationalism is somehow related to the ruling class. Of course, this is very simplified given the complexity of nationalism.
In 2007, I co-edited a book (with Minna Henriksson) called *Contemporary Art and Nationalism*. The idea was that nationalism is not a simple phenomenon. It is complex. And to grasp the complexity of nationalism, we must ask difficult questions. One of them is how nationalism finds its place within contemporary art. We usually think they exclude each other. So, in that sense, it seems very timely to pose the question of the nation in 1998, but even more important is that it is paired with money and the economy—that is, class. This is a pretty interesting approach. And I looked at the list of participants. You know, there are interesting names that today are not part of, let's say, the contemporary art world. Being from Kosovo, the only name from Kosovo that I could find is Jeta Xharra, today a famous investigative journalist, and also there is Želimir Žilnik, a militant filmmaker from Yugoslavia, whose work was mostly considered as documentary film in the first place. It is only after the mid 2000's that Žilnik's work was shown in the context of contemporary art. And, of course, there is the radio station, B92, today a mainstream nationalist media outlet, which in the '90s profited from anti-Milošević dissidentism. So, the whole affair is a bit complicated, as it always is with nationalism.

**Eleanor:**
I need to think a bit. Could you say in what way the politics
of border demarcation was a subject and how the creation of
alternative networks was practiced?

**Lucie:**
*MoneyNations* was about establishing links of exchange
between what was considered as the former "East" and the
"West" of Europe. These links should then form the infrastructural
foundation for a discourse on border policies in Europe and the
interconnectedness of capitalism, media and nationalism.
In the archive we found many letters from Marion and the team
writing to community centers, organizations or individuals in
an attempt to reach other voices and perspectives outside their
immediate western European realm in order to include them
in the project. It was about reflecting on the entanglement of
money and nationalism in Europe while actively attempting to
invest in the opposite—in narratives that don't perpetuate the
marginalization of the East. It's more a method we're interested
in, that seems to me to be also relevant in your respective
practices. More specifically: the relation between what you're
researching on or what texts you decide to publish and what
types of publics and production networks you create for that.

**Max:**
Marion was specifically reaching out to people in the former
Eastern bloc that were already working on or had already
developed media outlets, such as self-organized radio stations.
A big part of the whole project was, aside from the exhibition,
a three-day conference, including workshops where people got
together to share knowledge and strategies of self-organizing,
for instance. These were communication outlets that were
purposefully trying to subvert certain narratives propagated
by nation states. So, it was about resisting specific narratives
but also creating their own media outlets and information

channels. A big part of *MoneyNations* was communication
and networking among practitioners.

**Eleanor**:
It makes me think about internationalism, something that
we have spoken about and which is part of our publishing.
I suppose the kind of exchange that might happen between
different nation-states in the European Union is like a
centralized sort of quasi-internationalism. I'm interested in a
kind of internationalism that invests in alternative networks
and self-organized, self-determined connection between people
across borders. And the international is also within people.
States encourage us to suppress this through identification
with them. The question of how to have internationalist politics
is something that I'm very interested in thinking about.

**Jonas**:
Ferdi, would you like to add something?

**Ferdi**:
I see that we come from quite different backgrounds in
publishing and archiving. But I don't know where my practice
stands within this context, maybe more in the context of self-
organization. What I think is telling but also disheartening about
the thesis of *MoneyNations*, is that the agenda they criticized
continues today. Twentyfive years later, this logic is still part
of our reality. What is more, it has escalated, it has mutated
in terms of context, scale and complexity. To set the focus on
the relation between the West and the East of Europe at that
time could be understood as a simulation, a seed to what
would come in the following decades. I'm in a tricky position,
because I've been living in Germany for 11 years now. I'm trying
to navigate the borders that are addressed in the project, but
I'm also a part of it. I'm thinking of borders not only as, say,
a civic convention but also how they are embodied. When you

think about borders and control and surveillance, these figures
are located in the perimeter; but they are also institutional—
meaning they become the landscape of the institutions
that we're part of and thinking against. This is when it gets
complicated, because there's no outside. Like, we are all
in it but at the same time trying to work against it. This logic
is hard to undo. In the context of internationalization and
internationalism, I am reminded of *documenta 15*. There were
different politics in bringing artists doing self-organization to
Kassel, only to then be subjected again to these border politics
at the end.

**Jonas**:
This leads to another question we were asking ourselves,
which is why is the art field for all of us more or less our chosen
field of practice? in terms of organizing internationally or
working against those embodied forms of nationalisms, do
you think there is a specific potential in artistic publishing or
exhibition making?

**Eleanor**:
I am listening to a podcast called *Black Myths*. It's one of
the podcasts transcribed in Joy James' book *In Pursuit
of Revolutionary Love*. Recently, they did a double-episode
series with Vijay Prashad, an Indian-American historian. In
it, he speaks about the concept of the Third World, which was
originally a utopian idea and movement. It was really an act
of claiming; a term that was invented by countries who did not
see themselves as part of the so-called First World, nor as
part of the so-called Second World, which at the time was the
Soviet Union. The First World wanted to disqualify the political
challenge this Third World posed to its reign, and produced
propaganda accordingly. Hence it was only later that the
term "Third World" became derogatory and associated with
underdevelopment and poverty, etc. Third World was originally

a political proposition. In his interview, Prashad speaks a lot
about internationalism; that it makes sense only if you have
a collective idea of your political vision. He was talking about,
for example, connections between African-Americans and
Ghanaians, people struggling against racism in different
contexts as an example of a form of internationalism that made
sense because there was a shared wish for, say, communism
or revolution. But if the shared desire is not clear, then I wonder
on what grounds we connect or how we actually relate. That's
my feeling around your question of politics and art, it's almost
like the question is rather: What do we want in terms of the
material conditions of our life? And it is true that art is something
that we practice.

**Sezgin:**

I agree. Internationalism and the questions you raise, Eleanor,
are essential here. That would be a starting point. In the case
of my publishing practice, communism is a crucial subject.
I publish a lot on communism, but I am not interested in this
nostalgic idea of the "good" internationalism of the past, and
it's fundamental to keep in mind all the trauma of communism,
particularly Stalinism. The communism that I engage with is
one that complicates the common historical narratives, as in
the case of our book, *Free Jazz Communism* from 2019. It has
as its subject a concert of the Archie Shepp–Bill Dixon
Quartet at the 8th World Festival of Youth and Students in
Helsinki in 1962. This was a massive festival dedicated to
peace where 17,000 people attended, and it was organized
through the Eastern bloc. So, within the festival a concert of
the free jazz musicians Archie Shepp and Bill Dixon, as a
particular historical event, in itself distorts the Cold War
narrative as it is usually reproduced, where jazz music or
more generally Black music from the US, or art movements
like abstract expressionism, were interpreted as CIA cultural
propaganda. But these musicians came to play at a socialist-

left festival supported by Communist parties—in this case, the
CPUSA (Communist Party USA). So by digging and scratching
through archives and other traces of this event, we can see that
this common Cold War narrative is an ideological construction.
It also means that the ideological structures are not ubiquitous,
you know, they are not as strong as they look. I think it's also
one of Vijay Prashad's theses to say, yes, of course, there
is an internationalism, but there are these huge structures
in opposition to internationalism. To answer your first question
about methodologies: Rab-Rab Press is supporting publishing
that opposes the ideological narrative, which constantly repeats
the mantra that capitalism always wins. My work is about
opposing this assumption by pushing forward alternative ideas,
practices and historical events.

**Ferdi**:
I inhabit this space, the so-called art institution because it is
a space of possibilities, of being in relation with others. But,
on the other hand, when you think around this framework of
*MoneyNations*, and Sezgin, when you raise the question of
where that money is, you address exactly the core of what
makes things so complicated. Because the West is where the
money is. This, again, plays into the politics of invitations. Many
artists—or they might not even call themselves artists—from
parts of the Global South who are invited to come to Germany
or France or the Netherlands expect to explore these possibilities
of being in relation with others. But my concern is that capital
doesn't necessarily circulate; it stays within these spatial
boundaries and often doesn't really affect things back where
they are supposed to. This means to me that decentering is
then about redistributing this money, moving it around, rather
than keeping it; it's about bringing people at a certain location
together and then letting them go back to their own context.
At the same time, the money is still being kept within Fortress
Europe. So, I understand self-organization not as a work

directed against something; rather, it's for me about focusing on things that are important to a local context while neither engaging or disengaging from said structures. And if there's the need to be in relation or to collaborate, it can happen but it doesn't have to be the final aim. We should think about ways of doing things not within Europe, but in the context where it is needed.

**Eleanor:**
Going off what you just said, and keeping internationalism in mind, I have a question about why there is a need for Western European artists or curators to go somewhere else, retrieve something, and then bring it back to Europe. Like, it's not a given that this is how things go. Why isn't that research being done in Berlin or in Basel or in Brussels? There is a very strong European reflex to recuperate or co-opt what's happening somewhere else. So, with regards to internationalism, it's also about where you are and how you deal with things there.

**Sezgin:**
I would like to add a few thoughts with regards to redistribution that Ferdi brought up, and I think this also brings us back to the exhibition thesis of *MoneyNations*, as I understand it. Because although we have this dominant structure of the nation, money is per se an international thing. Money is very abstract as it's always global; Marx describes it in the first chapter of Capital as the most abstract of all values. In fact, money is what makes capitalism abstract and it's also what helps it in becoming immediately global; that is, capitalism does not have borders. It has to penetrate everywhere. Nevertheless, despite money and capitalism being global and not recognizing the borders, there are still all these nations with their borders within contemporary capitalism. I think this is a very uneasy question: how come we are not internationalist then? Why is the contemporary world still structured around

nationalist, particularist and very reactionary ideas? How are they reproduced within capitalism, which is driven by the violence of one class against another? It brings us to the question of whether there is such a thing as modernity when there's still today, and also throughout Europe, various archaic, presumably pre-capitalistic modes of production and exploitation. These very primitive modes of exploitation, nepotistic relationships, corruption and so on exist in the contemporary art world as well. This contradiction makes apparent the limits of conceiving emancipatory politics within contemporary art institutions.

**Jonas:**

I'm very interested in this European reflex that you, Eleanor, mentioned, of retrieving cultures or knowledge somewhere else. Taking that into account, how is it reflected in your own participation in the Western European art world? Do these questions play a role, when you publish radical authors such as, for example, Joy James?

**Eleanor:**

I came across Joy James' political theory through research into feminist and Black critiques of liberalism during my master's, though it wasn't taught by any professor in Belgium. We reached out to her initially wanting to republish one of her existing books, which are difficult to get hold of in Europe and the UK. The conversation led towards James proposing to publish a book of recent texts and mostly live interviews she'd been doing with podcasters, journalists, musicians, scholars and activists in the US and UK. So that book came about through their internationalist anti-racist struggle, which reached us. The USA and Europe are part of the international, of course. My personal relation to Europeanness is conflicted. I didn't grow up here, I come from Australia. I moved to Europe for work, basically. Although I have dealt with visa problems, immigrating to Europe was optional for me and my nationality, race and class facilitated that option. Obviously, in doing that, you inevitably affirm Europe as the center, whether or not you agree. Maybe my question about the need to look elsewhere has to do with this dilemma. So it's more this question of—and this is less about Marion von Osten than it is a general question to everyone—why is the culture where you are located not satisfactory, and what is this desire to go elsewhere? Like, what is it satisfying?

**Camilla:**
As a publisher we commission and distribute; that desire is definitely there. These things need to travel, they need to be distributed in different places. And in these practical questions of who you distribute with or the way we commission— especially after Brexit, because we're between the UK and Europe—we become infused with these contradictions as well. Would you agree, Eleanor?

**Eleanor:**
Yeah, totally. I think something great about the book format is that it can move and you don't need to. The approach that we take is very much focused on distribution.

**Lucie:**
In what way?

**Camilla:**
This is practical stuff, every book is costed, distribution first. We have a system set up, different channels our books go through to the public. I suppose, we consciously set up these channels thinking that the stuff that's circulating in the art world or academic worlds might be read more broadly, and hopefully distributed at a more accessible price. So, the commissioning and editing is informed by an awareness of how many copies

are going to be printed and where we want them to go. It's not abstract, the book comes into being in this kind of backwards way sometimes, distribution first.

**Jonas:**
There's another question I would like to ask Ferdi, which concerns *documenta 15*: did you feel like there was a common ground or a larger project that in that case was necessary for internationalism to happen?

**Ferdi:**
From what I heard, there are different forms of internationalism, and you can have an internationalism based on capital accumulation or based on solidarity. What I find interesting about *documenta* is the internationalism which is based on nationalism. A nationalist internationalism perhaps? I think it was Anselm Franke, who spoke about this obsession to become a world champion through these mega art events—to showcase international art in a certain way—while also claiming the power to be able to showcase, which goes against the idea of the kind of internationalism we were talking about. I'm more interested, for instance in the question of relation, and this is where the term transversality becomes important. There are examples within the international feminist movement, where the movement escalates without these kinds of extractivist relationships because the local context is so centered, but at the same time put in relation with other struggles. Verónica Gago writes about this in her book, *Feminist International: How to Change Everything*.
KUNCI, where I am a member, is part of a network called Arts Collaboratory, which includes 25 organizations in Latin America, the Middle East, Asia, Africa and Europe. We've been trying to think together about this question of money. While the money comes from Europe, we think about engaging with each other in a more equitable, non-exploitative way, and, related to this,

about strategies of decentering. We work against having one single controlling or regulating body. I guess Ruangrupa's lumbung at *documenta 15* was an attempt to invite *documenta* as an institution to be part of this kind of non-hierarchical way of doing art together, which apparently was not reciprocated.

**Lucie**:
It's great that you bring in Arts Collaboratory as an example for thinking about ways of redistributing and instituting networks differently. Going back to 1998, you sense a certain need to reflect on Europe and the narratives that mediate between East and West. In a way, I see *MoneyNations* as a very local initiative that tried to intervene in these narratives. But it still follows the logic of an institution which happens to be in the so-called West, that invites certain people to be part of it. I find it extremely inspiring to think about ways to avoid this particular pattern. Arts Collaboratory shows how essential it is to really think of entirely different organizational structures and funding schemes.

**Ferdi**:
The work with Arts Collaboratory is not easy at all; we've been functioning as a self-organized network since 2016, which adds up to seven years of doing things on the basis of these reflections and asking ourselves, "how to organize a translocal network in a self-organized way?" Also, the people involved work under very different conditions. Their political situations are so different, and so are the languages they speak. It's a constant negotiation. That's why it moves very slowly. But this is precisely the space I prefer to be in, rather than, you know, being in a space that is like a finished product. Productivity is understood differently in AC. After these many years, we are more concerned with building ethical ways of doing things together rather than, say, making exhibitions or other typical ways of "producing" art.

**Sezgin**:

I also think it's interesting to look at the difference between
*MoneyNations* and other exhibitions about Eastern Europe and
Yugoslavia—the Balkans, in particular—that took place just a few
years later, such as Harald Szeemann's *Blood and Honey* (2003,
Essl Museum, Klosterneuburg / Vienna) or René Block's *In the
Gorges of the Balkans* (2003, Kunsthalle Fridericianum, Kassel).
These exhibitions reflect the ideology of what was going on
in Berlin, Zurich or Vienna, because the break-up of the Eastern
bloc changed the whole of Europe's new conjuncture; the
1990s are dominated by this post-communist decay. But there
is another important historical shift that happened in the '90s.
And Marion von Osten—here also in terms of her other works,
engagements and projects—was aware of one very particular
contradiction, which is the following: these artists of the '90s
were all in favor of collective work pointing towards a new, more
egalitarian approach that would happen outside institutions and
that was a priori collaborative. As long as it remained outside
of this hierarchical, money-dominated, patriarchal, chauvinistic
context, it was genuinely collaborative in the new system of
democracy. But a contradiction appears regarding the Eastern
European countries that were, in fact, constitutively collective
because they were socialist. Let's remember that. From Poland
to Romania to Yugoslavia, all these countries were socialist.
They all had social ownership and collective labor written
into their respective constitutions, which means there was no
individual ownership. So, what sort of collectivity are we now
talking about when we discuss the failure of socialism? In
approaching this issue this tension generated a lot of different
intensities. And it becomes evident in curatorial practices
as well. I would like to mention one curatorial practice greatly
influenced by Marion von Osten, which is WHW (What, How
& for Whom). Their curatorial approach was an early reaction to
the complexities of the collective, how it existed in socialism,
and the dynamics of new collectives in a newly established

capitalism that in Yugoslavia was paired with nationalism.
WHW introduced the idea of a first and second collective with
a difference; the term "first collective" refers to the socialist
totalitarian collectivization of the state, while "second collective"
describes a new, progressive, liberal, open, innovative
collectivity practiced by these artists. That was their principal
thesis regarding the different types of collaborative practice
they undertook throughout the 2000s. Once you introduce this
second collective, you have already made the qualitative shift;
you have to follow the consequences of this theoretical position.
So there are differences in looking at the "other." Marion von
Osten's approach is different to Szeemann's is different to
WHW's or, for example, different from what Charles Esche
did in the early 2000s.

**Jonas**:
What are your thoughts on the term "counter-public", which
was used a lot to describe these politicized artistic practices
as they happened, for example, at the Shedhalle in Zurich?
Do you find the term "counter-public"—or, more generally,
an understanding of political work—to be directed against
something, still productive or helpful in any way?

**Ferdi**:
The concept of a counter-public is important to me. But it
comes with exhaustion, because you're trapped in this binary
logic of constantly working against something all the time.
Sometimes it also happens unintentionally, for example when
people work to support their communities, which then develops
into counter-works in the sense of creating counter-publics.
This has some merit, of course, but, again, the question would
be to what extent? I think it's rare, but some do succeed
in creating counter-narratives that are more sustainable. But
seen through the lens of power, histories have taught us how
what used to be counter-narratives then became hegemonic

narratives, which consequently instigate other counter-actions.
I don't want to sound too pessimistic, but I'm more invested
in what I mentioned much earlier regarding non-engagement,
or disengagement. For me, going sideways became more and
more important; sideways as a mode of working. Instead of
doing something in order to counter something else, it's more
about working with what is in front of you and what is needed.
And if a curator or an art institution would frame it as *counter*,
then so be it. Again, to me what is key is to focus on what's
on the ground, but also knowing that what's happening on
the ground is always happening in relation to something else.
Being a counter-agent is one way to do it. Sometimes this
kind of work can be inspiring, but most of the time it becomes
exhausting.

**Camilla**:
Counter is not something we've organized around, it has never
come up, it's not a term we've used for self-clarification. But
I recognize what you say, Ferdi … doing the work that's needed.
We often speak about "need" and trying to get into that zone.
It's almost like a physical place. In the writing we publish, the
experimental form comes out of a need. It's not decorative,
it's not on top of anything. The form of the writing comes from
a need and we try to edit in alignment with this need. That helps
to open it to a wider public, because we want to distribute
as widely as possible. So, centering the need is a way to make
the books open.

**Eleanor**:
Also, if you can name the counter-public, then it follows you
can name the public, and so you assume either that you're
not part of the public or that you know it totally. And those are
things that we would probably disagree with.

**Camilla:**

We often speak about how you can never know the reader. And that leads to a process of letting go of control. You cannot know the public; you cannot know what meaning the books will have or who is reading them. You can't edit or do anything in the process of making a book with an assumed public or meaning in your mind. Otherwise, you lose the thread of need.

**Sezgin:**

For me and my work with Rab-Rab, generating a counter-public or an alternative public is essential. Easier said than done. And, as Ferdi said, it is really exhausting. Rab-Rab works under certain ethical principles. One of these is that we don't publish the ready-made material or catalogs of institutions, we don't collaborate with art institutions according to their project-based administrated logic. Because our working ethic is founded on a belief that the subjectivity of our publishing practice is stronger than the objective conditions—no matter how much working with institutions might help the project to proliferate or gain wider distribution. This subjectivity generates a movement on its own, but it's not easy. Once you adopt an antagonistic relationship to the institution there is no way back. Publishing practice as a form of creating a counter-public has been discussed from the 1920s onwards, such as in the case of Karel Teige, whose writings we published. In fact, publishing—pamphlets, manifestos, whatever—is the first step of every political organization. We are currently working on a project called *Publishing as Scaffolding*. It comes from a description by Lenin, who wrote in 1902 about using new publishing forms to organize the working class. And he comes up with a metaphor, which is excellent, that publishing is like a scaffolding: it's a temporary structure to build the movement. You make it with very cheap materials and allow communication between different levels and components. And it's by definition collaborative and collective. ■

Material Marion von Osten 1
*MoneyNations*

Edited by:
Lucie Kolb
Jonas von Lenthe
Max Stocklosa

Including a
conversation with:
Sezgin Boynik
(Rab-Rab Press)
Ferdiansyah Thajib
(KUNCI Study
Forum & Collective)
Eleanor Ivory Weber
Camilla Wills
(Divided Publishing)

Copyediting:
Michael Baers

Proofreading:
Bram Opstelten

Design:
Max Stocklosa

Lithography:
Johann Hausstätter

Printed by:
druckhaus köthen

First edition, 600 copies
ISBN 978-3-948200-17-6

Published by:
Wirklichkeit Books
March 2024

www.wirklichkeitbooks.com
info@wirklichkeitbooks.com

Acknowledgments:
Peter Spillmann
Michael Zinganel
Natalie Seitz
Peter Riedlinger
Gülsün Karamustafa
Lina Grumm
Eleanor Ivory Weber
Camilla Wills
Ferdiansyah Thajib
Sezgin Boynik
Pauline Boudry
Schweizerisches Sozialarchiv

©2024 The artists, authors,
and photographers or their
legal successors and
Wirklichkeit Books.

Image credits:
Cover→Video still, Hi8 tape,
CPKC, Berlin
Page 110→Lia Perjovschi,
CPKC, Berlin

With the support of the Swiss
Arts Council Pro Helvetia

Editorial note:
The letters on pages 36–47
have been edited in terms
of punctuation, spelling and
grammar.

The artist, curator, researcher and educator Marion von
Osten (1963–2020) was based in Berlin since the early
1990s. Her transversal and always collaborative approach
manifested across various media, including exhibitions,
conferences, installations, as well as films, discussions,
texts, teachings or self-published journals. Her projects
were all intertwined and driven by her specific way
of working rooted in artistic research and feminist
organizing, with a transnational focus and a commitment
to the project of decolonization. Among her works are
the international exhibition series *bauhaus imaginista*
(2017–2019), *Viet Nam Discourse* (2016–2018) at Tensta
Konsthall, *Project Migration* (2002–2006) in Cologne,
and *Sex & Space* (1996) at Shedhalle Zurich. As collective
infrastructures, her collaborations included Labor k3000,
kleines postfordistisches Drama (Minor Post-Fordist
Drama, kpD) and the Center for Postcolonial Knowledge
and Culture (CPKC).

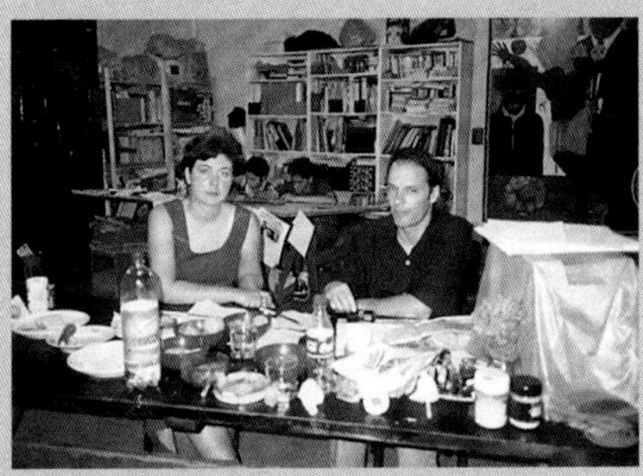

Marion von Osten and Peter Spillmann